101 PAPER-CRAFT Gift Ideas™

Edited by Vicki Blizzard

101 Paper-Craft Gift Ideas™

EDITOR Vicki Blizzard
ART DIRECTOR Brad Snow
PUBLISHING SERVICES MANAGER Brenda Gallmeyer
ASSOCIATE EDITOR Lisa M. Fosnaugh
ASSISTANT ART DIRECTOR Nick Pierce
COPY SUPERVISOR Michelle Beck
COPY EDITORS Nicki Lehman, Mary O'Donnell, Beverly Richardson
TECHNICAL EDITOR Läna Schurb
PHOTOGRAPHY Justin & Kelly Wiard
GRAPHIC ARTS SUPERVISOR Ronda Bechinski
COVER DESIGN Erin Augsburger
GRAPHIC ARTIST Joanne Gonzalez
PRODUCTION ASSISTANTS Cheryl Kempf, Marj Morgan
TECHNICAL ARTISTS Nicole Gage, Liz Morgan

CHIEF EXECUTIVE OFFICER John Robinson
PUBLISHING DIRECTOR David J. McKee
BOOK MARKETING DIRECTOR Craig Scott
EDITORIAL DIRECTOR Vivian Rothe

Printed in China
First Printing: 2005
Library of Congress Control Number: 2005920782
Hardcover ISBN: 1-59217-062-5
Softcover ISBN: 1-59217-087-0

Dear Crafter,

Crafting with paper is so popular right now, and you can do such wonderful things with it. In this book we'll show you 101 different things you can do with paper, and they all make great gift ideas.

If you're a scrapbooker, you probably have everything you need on hand: punches, die cuts, decorative-edge scissors and markers. If you're a general crafter, you will have a good portion of the products you need: paint, brushes, sealers, surfaces and adhesives—just add paper and a few other basic tools to get started on fun craft projects!

We've included ideas for all sorts of gift-giving occasions throughout the year. Many of the projects, while gifts themselves, also serve as gift containers. Altered tins hold photo CDs, baskets and gift jars are keepsake projects that hold handmade treats, little boxes will hold special gifts and will also hold mementoes and other small treasures after the gift is opened.

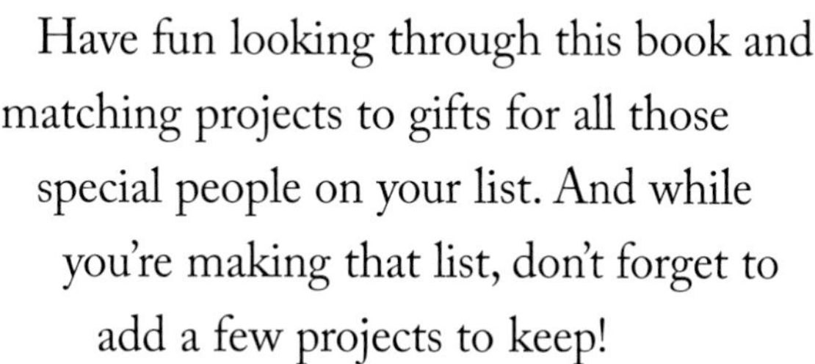

Have fun looking through this book and matching projects to gifts for all those special people on your list. And while you're making that list, don't forget to add a few projects to keep!

Warm regards,

Contents

July Through September

Carry over the excitement of a Fourth-of-July fireworks show with a festive gift that's perfect all summer. **Page 86**

October Through December

Halloween, Thanksgiving, Christmas—so many reasons to give a gift! You'll love the choices filling this chapter. **Page 120**

January Through March

Delight the special people in your life with thoughtful gifts during the winter months. Crafting with paper is a sure way to beat the winter blues, and handcrafted gifts are always appreciated!

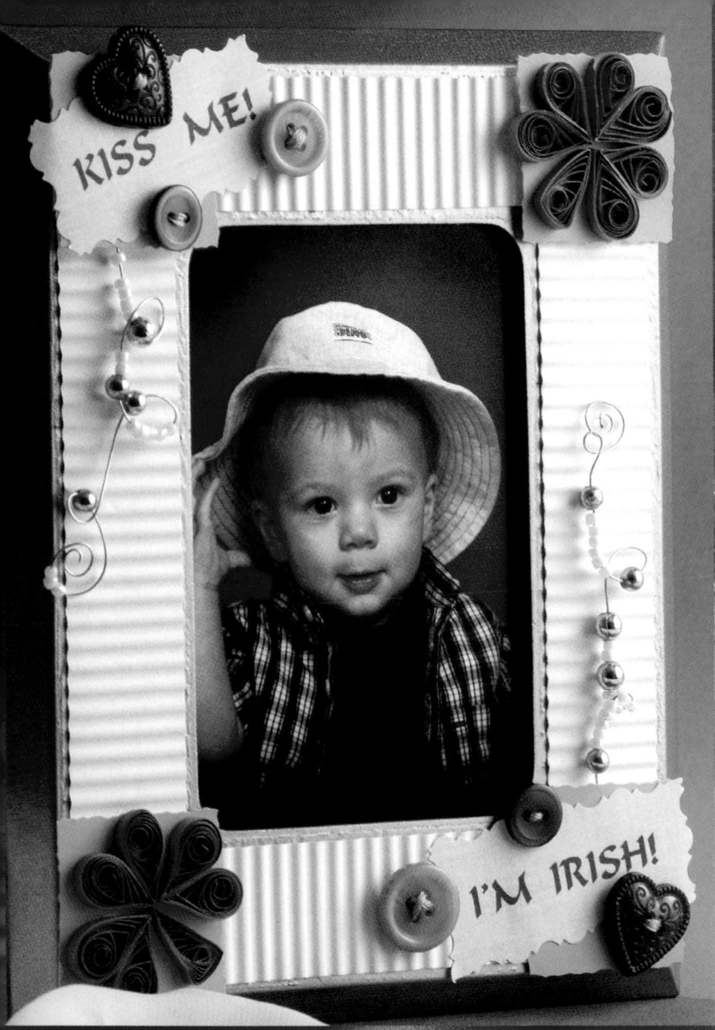

A Valentine Message

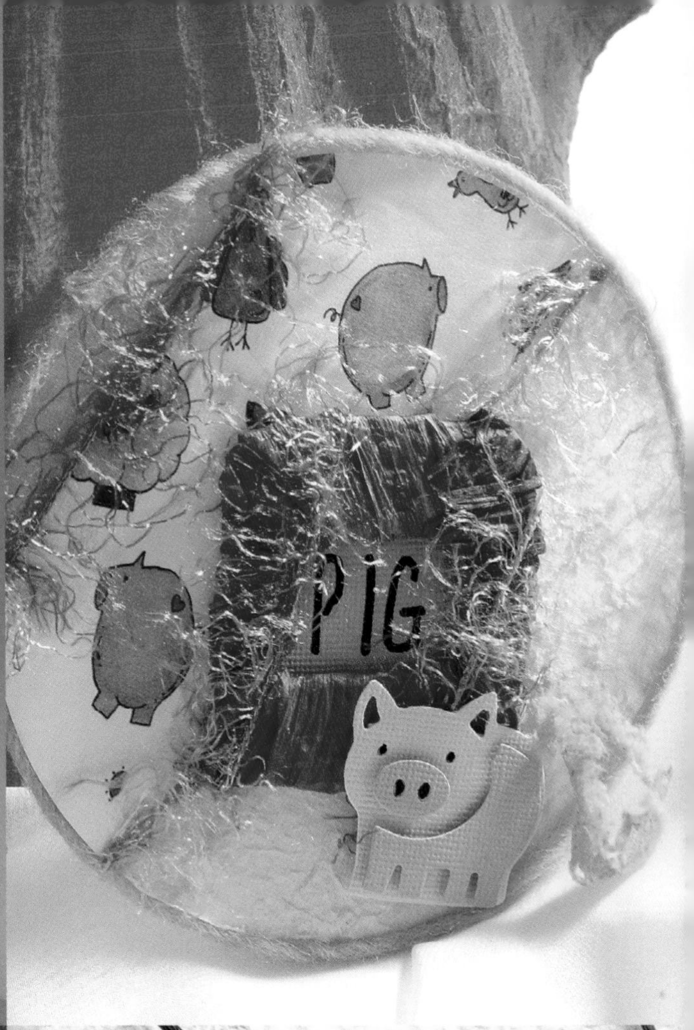

Happy St. Patrick's Day
1995

2005
ne minute to midnight
One minute to go
One minute to say good-bye
efore we say hello
Let's start the new year right
Twelve o'clock tonight
When they dim the light, let's begin
Kissing the old year out
Kissing the new year in
Let's watch the old year die
With a fond good-bye
And our hopes as high as a kite
How can our love go wrong if
start the new year right?
Happy
New Years

Happy New Year CD

Design by SUSAN STRINGFELLOW

Welcome the new year with an altered CD magnet complete with lyrics to a favorite song.

Thoroughly sand surface of CD with sandpaper so that glue will adhere. Use computer or hand print song lyrics on ivory card stock so that it will fit on the right side of the CD. Lay CD over lyrics; cut out lyrics with craft knife. Adhere lyrics to CD with clear-drying glue. Cut a piece of clock-pattern paper to fit over left side of CD; adhere to CD with clear-drying glue. Rub edges of CD over brown ink pad. Stamp brown and black vintage ornamental designs around the edges of the ivory card stock.

Use computer or hand print "Happy New Years" on wheat card stock to fit in ⅞ x 1⅜-inch rectangle; cut out. Rub edges of rectangle over brown ink pad. Adhere rectangle to lower left side of CD with glue stick.

Adhere a 5-inch piece of decorative fiber to seam between clock-pattern paper and song lyrics with paper glaze; glue ends on back. Knot 2- to 3-inch pieces of fiber through holes in "Celebrate" tag; glue tag and heart buttons to left side of CD with paper glaze. Glue ends of fiber on back. Attach star clip over right edge of CD.

Use computer or hand print "2005" *reversed* on scrap paper. Adhere to black card stock; cut out numerals with craft knife. Transfer gold rub-on finish to front of black numerals; adhere numerals along upper left edge of CD with glue stick, overlapping edge.

Crumple calendar pages; spray with walnut ink and rub surface over brown ink pad. Adhere pages to back of CD along upper right edge with clear-drying glue. Peel backing from magnet strips; adhere to back of CD. ■

SOURCES: Vintage patterned paper from Deluxe Designs; rubber stamps from Making Memories; star clip and walnut ink spray from Altered Pages; Diamond Glaze from JudiKins.

MATERIALS

- Blank CD
- Card stock: ivory, black and textured wheat
- Vintage-clock-patterned paper
- November and December pages from small 2004 calendar
- Scrap paper
- Rubber stamp with curved vintage design
- Ink pads: brown and black
- Walnut ink spray
- Star paper clip
- Metallic gold rub-on finish
- "Celebrate" metal tag
- 2 heart buttons
- Decorative fiber
- Adhesive-backed magnet strips
- Sandpaper
- Craft knife
- Lyrics to a New-Year themed song
- Glue stick
- Clear-drying glue
- Paper glaze
- Computer fonts (optional)

New Year Shaker Tag

Design by SUSAN HUBER

Attach this fun gift tag to the front of a sparkling-beverage bottle to help your hostess ring in the New Year!

Cut silver sparkle handmade paper the same size as manila tag; adhere with paper glue. Color tag edges with silver leafing pen. Thread fibers through hole in tag; knot.

Cut a 1¾ x ¾-inch window in bottle die cut with craft knife. Cut acetate slightly larger to cover window; glue to wrong side of die cut. Trace around die cut onto foam-core board; cut out. Cut a window in center of foam-core bottle, making it slightly larger than window in die cut.

Trace around bottle die cut onto green card stock; cut out. Glue to back of foam-core bottle. Pour beads into cutout opening in foam-core bottle. Glue bottle die cut on top, enclosing beads. Glue gold sparkle ribbon around edges of bottle.

Accent "celebrate" silver tag with metallic marking pens. Tie "celebrate" silver tag around neck of bottle with decorative fibers. Glue bottle to manila tag. Outline edges of bottle with gold metallic marking pen. Punch out letter tiles to spell "New Year." Attach letter tiles to manila tag with frame fasteners. ■

SOURCES: Leafing pen from Krylon; marking pens from Uchida of America; tag from Eyelet Queen; letter tiles and square frame fasteners from Scrapworks.

MATERIALS

- Manila paper tag
- Silver sparkle handmade paper
- Green card stock
- Champagne bottle die cut
- Foam-core board
- Clear acetate
- Silver leafing pen
- Metallic marking pens
- Complementary seed beads
- "Celebrate" silver tag
- Letter tiles
- Tiny square frame fasteners
- Decorative fibers
- ⅛-inch-wide gold sparkle ribbon
- Craft knife
- Paper glue

Happy New Year Votives

Designs by MARY AYRES

Ring in the New Year with the light of these glittery votive candleholders.

MATERIALS

- Glass votive candleholder
- White votive candle
- Card stock: white, light blue, bright blue, light purple, bright purple, light green and bright green
- 2 silver eyelets and eyelet-setting tool
- Green or blue decorative fibers
- 8mm sequins: 1 each green, blue and purple
- Ultrafine iridescent glitter
- New Year's Eve rub-on transfers
- Silver ink pad
- Decorative punches: swirl, ½-inch circle, spiral and flower
- ⅛-inch circle punch
- Small piece of sponge
- Instant-dry paper glue
- Jewel glue

***Project note:** Use instant-dry paper glue unless instructed otherwise.*

Tear a 2½ x 1½-inch rectangle from white card stock; ink edges. Lightly dab jewel glue around edges with sponge; sprinkle with glitter. Tap off "excess;" let dry.

Punch a ⅛-inch hole in each side near edge; set eyelets in holes. Adhere transfer to center of rectangle.

Punch a shape from each light color of card stock. Adhere shapes around transfer; glue a matching sequin to each. Punch a shape from each bright color of card stock. Glue between other shapes.

Thread a strand of fiber through each eyelet. Glue card stock to candleholder. Tie ends of fibers on back. ■

SOURCES: Decorative punches from EK Success; rub-on transfers from Royal & Langnickel; instant-dry paper glue and jewel glue from Beacon.

Hanging Snowflake Candle Votive

Design by SANDY ROLLINGER

Enjoy snowflakes without the wintry chill with light from this embellished votive holder.

Cut a 3-inch-wide strip of vellum long enough to go around votive holder plus ¼ inch. Randomly stamp snowflake image on vellum with white embossing ink; apply white sparkle powder and emboss. Trim bottom edge of vellum with decorative-edge scissors; set aside.

Wrap silver wire around top edge of votive holder. Using needle-nose pliers, twist wire into a loop on two sides, making sure wire is wrapped tightly around holder. Adhere double-stick tape to bottom edge of votive holder. Cut beaded fringe long enough to wrap around bottom edge and press fringe onto tape.

Cut six 3-inch pieces of wire. Curl one end of each piece in a spiral; slide three round beads and three bugle beads onto wire, alternating round and bugle shapes. Curl straight end of wire in a loose "S" shape.

Adhere double-stick tape around top edge of votive, over wire. Press top edge of vellum onto tape and wrap around votive. Add a piece of double-stick tape where vellum overlaps in back; press seam together. Adhere double-stick foam tape around rim of votive, over vellum.

Cut another piece of vellum. Apply white embossing ink to it. Pour on embossing powder and emboss. Punch several snowflakes from embossed vellum.

Press beaded wires ½ inch apart along top edge of foam tape. Press an embossed snowflake over each wire. Apply a light layer of glitter to exposed foam tape.

Cut a 10-inch piece of wire; fold it in half and form a hanging loop at top. Insert ends through side loops; wrap wire twice around each loop to secure. Add beads to wire ends; curl wires to hold beads in place. ■

MATERIALS

- White vellum
- Decorative-edge scissors
- 2½-inch-tall glass votive holder
- Small snowflake punch
- Small snowflake rubber stamp
- White sparkle embossing powder
- White embossing ink
- Silver and clear beaded fringe
- Fine glitter
- Silver bugle and iridescent round beads
- 20-gauge silver wire
- Needle-nose pliers
- Wire cutters
- Heat embossing tool
- ½-inch craft brush
- ¼-inch white double-stick foam tape
- ¼-inch double-stick adhesive tape

Winter CD Case

Design by MAUREEN SPELL

Metal snowflakes and fuzzy fibers accent the front of a case created just to hold a photo CD filled with precious winter memories.

***Project note:** Adhere elements with craft cement unless otherwise instructed.*

Remove packaging inserts from CD case; save to use for template. Cut two pieces of block-pattern paper approximately 4¾ inches square for front and back covers. Transfer alphabet rub-ons to upper left quadrant of front cover to spell "Winter." Insert front cover into front of CD case. Cut a 4¾ x ¾-inch strip of red card stock; slip it into spine of CD case. Adhere back cover to back of CD case with craft cement.

Brush white paint over metal frame. Immediately wipe off excess paint with paper towel, leaving color in the crevices. Cut a 2-inch square of red card stock; adhere to back of frame. Place glittery white fiber in the organza bag; wrap ribbon ties around neck of bag and tie. Adhere bag to card stock in center of frame using strong, double-stick adhesive tape.

Adhere a rhinestone in the center of each metal snowflake. Arrange snowflakes on front of CD case without gluing them down; lay framed arrangement in center, overlapping snowflakes. Adhere snowflakes to back of frame with strong, double-stick adhesive tape. Adhere entire frame collage to front of CD case with strong, double-stick adhesive tape. Wrap glittery white fiber around front cover of CD case, next to spine; knot ends. ■

SOURCES: Patterned paper from American Crafts; metal frame, snowflakes and rub-on transfers from Making Memories.

MATERIALS

- CD case with clear lid
- Red card stock
- Winter-block-pattern paper
- 2⁵⁄₁₆-inch-square metal winter frame
- 2 (1½-inch) metal snowflakes
- White alphabet rub-on transfers
- Glittery white fiber
- 2-inch white organza bag with white satin ribbon ties
- White acrylic paint
- 2 clear round rhinestones
- Paintbrush
- Paper towels
- Craft cement
- Double-stick adhesive tape

Enchanting Opalescent Box

Design by DEBBIE RINES, COURTESY OF DUNCAN

A simple papier-mâché box covered with mulberry paper is instantly transformed into a lovingly created gift.

Remove lid from box. Apply a thin, even coat of glue to bottom and sides of box. Carefully adhere mulberry paper; wrap over top edges and cut off excess.

Cut a piece of mulberry paper several inches larger than top of lid; crumple paper into a ball and slowly open it. Smooth paper slightly. Apply glue to top and sides of lid; center and adhere paper on lid. Wrap paper around sides and to inside edges; apply glue to adhere. Cut off excess.

Sponge white paint onto box; while paint is still wet, sponge light blue paint on top of white. Use a larger amount of light blue paint on bottom of box; let dry.

Paint a thin light blue line along scallops, ¼ inch from edge. Adhere a round stone in center of lid with light blue opalescent paint; apply 10 dots of light blue and light purple opalescent paint around stone. Using light purple opalescent paint, adhere five oval stones around center stone to form a flower shape.

Adhere a round stone on each corner of lid with light purple opalescent paint; apply a dot of light blue opalescent paint beside each corner stone. Let paint dry before proceeding to side of lid.

Using light blue opalescent paint, adhere two round stones on each side of lid at both ends; apply light purple opalescent dots at each scallop. ***Note:*** *Let one side dry before moving on to the next.* ■

SOURCES: Stones and paint from Duncan.

MATERIALS

- Oval and round clear stones
- White mulberry paper
- Acrylic paint: light blue and white
- Opalescent dimensional paint: light blue and light purple
- Papier-mâché box with scallop-edge lid
- Paintbrushes
- Craft sponge
- Thin tacky glue

Groundhog Day Frame

Design by SANDY ROLLINGER

Surround a photo of loved ones with the shadow of spring and a grinning groundhog friend.

Paint frame with two coats gesso using foam brush; dry after each coat.

Blend flow medium into a puddle of blue paint. Lightly blend in a small amount of pearl white, leaving some streaks. Sponge mixture across top three-quarters of frame for sky, leaving some white streaks visible. Let dry.

Blend flow medium into a puddle of green paint. Add a little white to make lighter green. Sponge mixture across bottom quarter of frame for grass; let dry.

Squeeze jagged lines of green paint straight from bottle for weeds and grass clumps. Squeeze three taller stems with leaves up right side of frame. Let dry.

Cut groundhog from brown card stock, tummy from tan, and shadow and hole from black. From tan punch one heart for muzzle and two ¼-inch circles for inner ears. Glue heart upside-down to face; glue circles in ears and tummy to body. Glue hole and shadow onto back of groundhog (check fit on frame).

Dot on eyes with black paint; add larger oval for nose; dot specks onto muzzle. Add fur details with gold paint. Dot on teeth with white. Let dry. Add smile and outline teeth with black permanent pen. Dot white highlight onto nose; let dry. Glue groundhog with shadow and hole in lower left corner of frame.

Punch 1-inch circle from yellow for sun; cut ⅛-inch slice off left edge. Cut rays from yellow; glue sun on top of rays. Glue sun to frame in upper left corner.

Punch flowers from orange card stock. Glue to tops of stems and in grass. Dot purple paint in flower centers. Squeeze jagged lines of green paint overlapping edge of shadow. Let dry.

Write "Me … and my shadow" across top of frame with black permanent pen. ■

SOURCES: Paints from Plaid; instant-dry paper glue from Beacon.

DRAWINGS on page 156

MATERIALS

- 8½ x 6½-inch wooden frame
- Gesso
- Opaque paper paints: blue, purple, black and green
- White and metallic and gold metallic paper paints
- Flow medium
- Card stock: yellow, brown, tan, black and orange
- Paper punches: heart, flower, ¼-inch and 1-inch circles
- ½-inch foam brush
- Small piece of sponge
- Black fine-tip permanent pen
- Instant-dry paper glue

Pop-up Groundhog Day Card

Design by MARY AYRES

Surprise someone special with a pop-up groundhog who wishes for spring!

Form a 5 x 7-inch card from light blue card stock.

Use computer and font or hand print "happy groundhog" on light turquoise card stock. Tear a 4½ x 3¾-inch rectangle around words; rub edges with blue ink pad. Glue to top front of card. Use computer and font or hand print "day" on tan card stock. Tear a 4½ x 2¾-inch rectangle with word at center bottom; ink edges with brown ink. Glue to bottom front of card, overlapping turquoise. Using pattern provided, cut hole from black card stock; glue to front of card.

Cut a 4½ x 6½-inch rectangle from light turquoise card stock. Ink edges with blue ink.

CONTINUED on page 27

MATERIALS

- Card stock: white, tan, medium brown, black, yellow, orange, light blue and light turquoise
- Dye ink pads: blue and brown
- Decorative punches: ½-inch and 1¼-inch circles, 1-inch seal
- Black fine-tip permanent marker
- Decorative-edge scissors
- Rotary tool and scoring blade (optional)
- Instant-dry paper glue
- Computer fonts (optional)

Sweet Sounds CD Holder

Design by HEATHER D. WHITE

Surprise your sweetie with a personalized CD filled with songs that are special only to the two of you, and present it in an embellished holder!

Project notes: *Adhere all papers and other elements with double-sided tape. Rub dark brown ink pad across edges and surfaces of all patterned paper pieces for an antiqued effect.*

Cover front and back flaps of CD folder with dark red checked paper. Cover inside of CD folder with separate squares of dark red checked paper.

Center and adhere one 4¾-inch square of wheat grass striped paper on front cover. Center and adhere one 4½-inch square of dark red vines paper to wheat grass square. Measure heart paper border sticker to fit across front cover. Ink edges; adhere sticker about 7⁄16 inch from bottom.

Adhere title to CD folder using tag, stickers and charm. ■

SOURCES: Journal/CD folder from Pine Cone Press; patterned papers, metal tag, stickers and charms from All My Memories.

MATERIALS

- Single pocket journal/CD folder
- Patterned papers: dark red checks and vines, and wheat grass stripes
- Printed heart paper border sticker
- Metal "sweet" tag
- Silver-trimmed typewriter-key letter stickers
- Silver steel typewriter letter stickers
- Gunmetal oval "Love" charm
- Dark brown pigment ink pad
- Double-sided tape

Love Book

Design by STACEY WAKELIN

Spell out your feelings for a loved one on the pages of a book kit by using a variety of stickers and embellishments!

MATERIALS

Book kit
Coordinating patterned papers
12 inches natural raffia
Assorted metal embellishments
Assorted alphabet stickers and letter tiles
Brown dye ink pad
Photos
¼-inch circle punch
Glue stick
Craft cement
Double-sided adhesive squares
Adhesive foam dots

Cover book covers with printed paper using glue stick. Cover each inside sheet with a coordinating piece of printed paper using glue stick. Ink edges of covers and pages for an antiqued look.

Assemble book by punching holes in each page and in the cover. Tie pages and covers together with raffia.

Embellish pages and covers as desired. Use an assortment of dimensional letters, stickers and photographs for each page, using project photos as an inspiration. ■

SOURCES: Book kit from Halcraft.

How Lucky Am I Accordion Book

Design by HEATHER D. WHITE

Create a very personal tribute to a loved one by filling the pages of an accordion book with cherished photos and sweet sentiments!

MATERIALS

3¾ x 4½-inch blank accordion book
Green block printed paper background sheets
Green patterned papers
Bronze charms: heart and square
Bronze medium accent bar
Assorted alphabet stickers
Word stickers
Twill word stickers
Word rub-on transfers
Green brads
Green eyelets and eyelet-setting tool
Bronze extra large square brads
Sepia-tone photos
Dark brown pigment ink pad
Double-sided tape

Project note: *Adhere all papers and other elements with double-sided tape.*

Cut a piece from a green block printed background sheet to use as background for accordion book cover. Ink edges and surface of background. Cut coordinating patterned papers to fit in sections of block printed background sheet. Ink edges and surfaces. Adhere patterned papers to background sheet.

Cut a photo mat for book cover from another block printed background sheet. Ink edges and surface. Adhere photo mat at an angle to left side of block printed background sheet. Cut photo slightly smaller than photo mat; adhere photo to mat.

Add title to accordion book cover using assorted word rub-on transfers, word labels and letter stickers adhered to bronze accent bars and extra-large brads, and green brads to indicate ellipses and other punctuation. Center and adhere entire cover arrangement to cover of book.

Measure and cut coordinating patterned papers for backgrounds for each of the accordion book's six inner pages. Ink edges and surfaces. To add variety, use torn strips, double matting, etc. ***Note:*** *You need not coordinate facing pages; however, on sample, each two-page pair features a mirror image of the design for that pair.*

Once page backgrounds are complete, add titles and words using assorted stickers, rub-on transfers, bronze brads, eyelets, accent bars, etc. Add bronze charms and other accents as desired. For each photo page, cut a photo mat from a background sheet. Ink edges and surface. Adhere photo mat to page background. Cut photo slightly smaller than photo mat; adhere photo to mat. Adhere entire arrangement to page.

Cut a piece from a block printed background sheet to cover back cover of accordion book. Ink edges and surface of background; adhere to back cover.

Optional: For a finished look, measure and cut a coordinating blank piece of block printed background paper for the back of each page. Ink edges and surfaces; adhere to backs of pages. ■

SOURCES: Accordion book from K&Company; embellishments from All My Memories and Making Memories.

Filigree Heart Container

Design by SANDY ROLLINGER

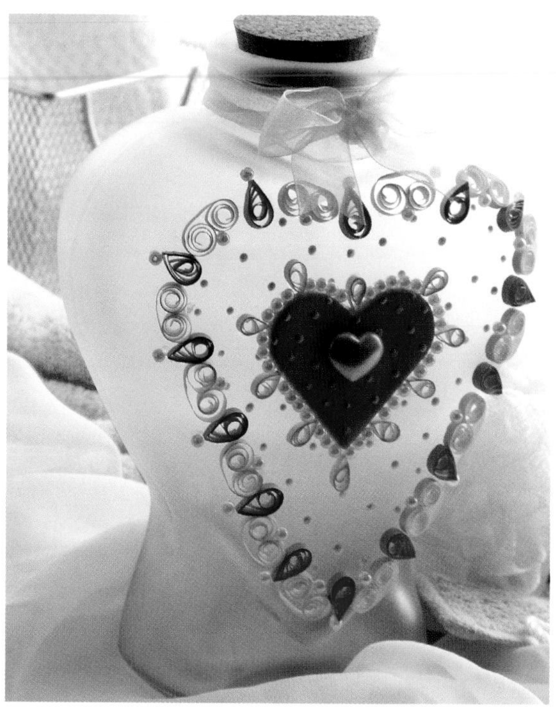

Delicate paper coils surround a pearl-embellished heart on the front of this romantic container. Fill with bath salts for an extra-special gift.

Project notes: *Glue ends of quilled paper strips with paper glue to secure individual shapes. Refer to photo for placement of quilled shapes on container. Use tweezers to position shapes. Use instant-dry glue for attaching quilled papers, heart and beads to container.*

Clean container with glass cleaner and soft cloth. Let dry. Spray container with several light coats of frosted glass spray, letting spray dry between coats.

Blend a tiny ball of red modeling compound into a larger ball of white to make pink. Roll out ¼ inch thick with brayer. Cut heart with cookie cutter; let dry for a few hours.

Cut 14 (4-inch) strips each of pink and white quilling paper. Roll each pink strip into a teardrop shape. Roll each white strip into a "C" scroll. Cut 10 (2-inch) strips of white quilling paper. Roll each into a teardrop shape.

Glue pink heart in center of container. Remove shank from button with wire cutters. Glue button to heart with quick-drying glue. Randomly add dots of white pearl paint to heart and container. Let dry.

Glue small white teardrops around heart. Begin by gluing one at the upper edge of the heart, one at the bottom point, and others around heart. Leave room to add pearls. Glue pearls around heart between teardrops. Let dry.

Glue one pink teardrop to jar with point pointing toward top of jar. Alternate gluing pink teardrops and white "C" scrolls around shape of jar. Leave at least ½ inch between heart and quilled shapes in border.

Glue pearls to points of pink teardrops and to "C" scrolls where coils meet. Let dry.

Tie ribbon around neck of container. Fill bottle with bath salts, bath oil, potpourri or candy. ■

SOURCES: Glass finish from Krylon; Delight air-dry modeling compound from Creative Paperclay Co. Inc.; paque paper paint from Plaid; instant-dry paper glue and paper glue from Beacon.

DRAWINGS on page 158

MATERIALS

- 5 x 7-inch flat-sided glass container with stopper
- White frosted glass spray
- Air-dry modeling compound: white and red
- ½-inch white pearl shank button
- Metallic pearl white paper paint
- ⅛-inch-wide paper quilling strips: pink and white
- 4mm white pearls
- ½-inch-wide white organza ribbon
- Glass cleaner
- Soft cloth
- 2-inch heart cookie cutter
- Acrylic brayer or roller
- Slotted quilling tool
- Wire cutter
- Toothpicks
- Tweezers
- Instant-dry paper glue
- Paper glue

Valentine Tin

Design by EILEEN HULL

Use a fun lettering font to create a play on words on the front of your valentine's can of treats.

MATERIALS

New, clean, quart paint can with lid
3 or 4 sheets coordinating scrapbooking paper
White vellum
Decorative-edge scissors
Heart punch
Computer font (optional)
Double-sided tape
Spray adhesive

Cut scrapbooking paper to fit around can, piecing as needed. Adhere paper to can using spray adhesive or double-sided tape.

Use computer or hand print "I CAN not live without you" on vellum to fit within a 2½ x 2-inch rectangle. Cut out rectangle with decorative-edge scissors.

Cut a 3 x 2½-inch rectangle from coordinating paper. Adhere vellum in center using spray adhesive. Cut a 3¼ x 2¾-inch rectangle from another paper. Adhere to vellum and first rectangle with double-sided tape. Adhere to can with double-sided tape.

Use computer or hand print "Be my Valentine" around edges of a 3-inch circle of paper. Trim edges with decorative-edge scissors to fit on lid. Punch heart in center of circle. Tape another piece of paper behind heart cutout. Adhere paper to lid with spray adhesive or double-sided tape. ■

Heart Songs

Design by HEATHER D. WHITE

Count the ways you love someone with sentiments from the heart nestled inside a tiny, paper-covered box!

Cut music-patterned paper to fit lid and box, including bottom of box. Ink paper to antique. Adhere paper to lid and box with double-sided tape.

Add message to box lid with domed stickers, rub-on transfers, sticker labels and cutouts.

Fill box with loving messages written on small pieces of paper, candy or other treats. ■

SOURCES: Patterned paper and alphabet stickers from Rusty Pickle; rub-on transfers from Making Memories; other stickers and embellishments from Pebbles Inc.

MATERIALS

- Heart-shaped papier-mâché box with lid
- Vintage music–patterned paper
- Domed alphabet stickers
- Word rub-on transfers
- Love sticker labels
- Love paper cutouts
- Black ink pad
- Double-sided tape

Love & Hearts CD

Design by SUSAN HUBER

Fringy fiber and wire add eye-catching flair to this otherwise simple CD.

MATERIALS

Blank CD
Card stock: black and deep red
Red mulberry paper
2 dark red primitive heart die cuts
1-inch red self-adhesive letter tiles to spell "LOVE"
Love collage rubber stamp
White ink pad
Red fringed fiber
¼-inch-wide red gingham ribbon
¼-inch-wide red satin picot-edge ribbon
White craft wire
Sandpaper
Craft knife
Wire cutters
Tweezers
Foam tape
Clear-drying glue

Project note: *Adhere elements with clear-drying glue unless otherwise instructed.*

Thoroughly sand front and back surfaces of CD with sandpaper so that glue will adhere. Stamp black card stock with love collage stamp and white ink. Lay CD over stamped words; cut a piece large enough to cover right three-quarters of CD with craft knife. Adhere black card stock to CD. Lay CD over red mulberry paper; cut a piece large enough to cover left one-third of CD with craft knife. Tear mulberry paper along right edge; adhere mulberry paper to CD, overlapping black card stock.

Glue red gingham ribbon across bottom of CD 1 inch from edge. Adhere letter tiles in a square on left side of CD. Lay red fringed fiber down CD between rows of tiles; glue ends of red fringed fiber on back of CD. Cut two 4-inch pieces of white wire. Wrap each piece around a red heart die cut; bend and curl wire ends with tweezers. Adhere wires to backs of die cuts with adhesive foam dots. Peel remaining backing from adhesive dots; adhere heart die cuts and wires to card, overlapping hearts slightly.

Cut a 2-inch piece of red gingham ribbon; bend in half and glue cut ends to wrong side of CD at center top with loop extending ½ inch. Thread picot-edge ribbon through loop; tie in a bow. Cut dark red card stock to cover CD; glue to back of CD. ■

SOURCES: Die cuts from QuicKutz; epoxy tiles from Tiles Play; rubber stamp from Paper Inspirations; wire from Artistic Wire.

love
and
XO
XO
kisses

Love & Kisses Frame

Design by HEATHER D. WHITE

Torn paper and sanded edges create a trendy, distressed look on the front of this paper-covered wooden frame.

Cut barnwood red patterned paper to fit front, back and edges of frame, including edges around photo opening. Lightly sand edges and surfaces of paper with sandpaper. Adhere paper to frame with double-sided tape.

Tear an 8 x 3½-inch strip barnwood willow patterned paper and an 8 x 4-inch strip of words-patterned paper. With scissors, trim both strips to fit around photo opening. Lightly sand edges and surfaces of paper with sandpaper. Adhere words-patterned paper to frame with double-sided tape. Adhere barnwood willow patterned paper over words-patterned paper with double-sided tape.

Arrange cutouts, and cut and torn pieces of patterned paper on front of frame. Lightly sand edges and surfaces of cutouts and patterned-paper pieces with sandpaper. Adhere cutouts and patterned-paper pieces to frame with double-sided tape. ■

SOURCES: Patterned papers and paper cutouts from Pebbles Inc..

MATERIALS

- 8-inch-square wooden frame
- Patterned papers: barnwood red, barnwood willow and words
- Love paper cutouts
- Black ink pad
- Sandpaper
- Double-sided tape

Pop-up Groundhog Day Card

CONTINUED FROM PAGE 17

Glue rectangle inside card on left side. Using pattern provided, cut ground rectangle from tan card stock; tear along top edge. Ink edges with brown ink. Score and fold rectangle along vertical center line, folding V to inside. Apply glue only along side edges of rectangle; adhere inside card ½ inch from bottom and sides. (Rectangle will not lie flat against card at center.)

Using pattern provided, cut groundhog from brown card stock. Add eyes and mouth with marker. Punch ½-inch black circle for nose; glue to groundhog. Glue bottom edge of groundhog to left side of V section.

Punch 1-inch seal from yellow card stock; punch 1¼-inch circle from orange. Glue seal to circle; glue circle in upper left corner. Using pattern provided, cut cloud circle from white card stock using decorative-edge scissors. Cut circle in

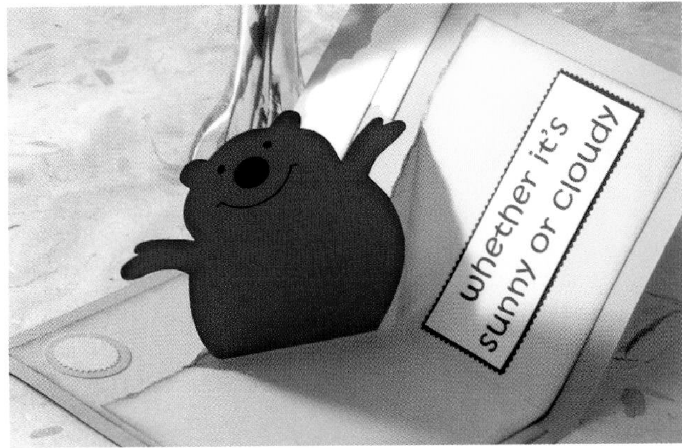

half with regular scissors; overlap pieces and glue in upper right corner.

Use computer and font or hand print "whether it's sunny or cloudy" on white card stock to fit in a 4 x 1½-inch rectangle. Mat with black card stock; trim with decorative-edge scissors. Glue inside card at bottom right. ■

SOURCES: Instant-dry paper glue from Beacon; seal punches from All Night Media/Plaid.

DRAWINGS on page 156

sara & chris
Forever
TRUE LOVE

True Love Frame

Design by MARY AYRES

Motifs cut from embossed paper are surrounded by popular slide mounts to create a photo frame that celebrates true love.

***Project note:** Assemble all components using instant-dry glue.*

Use a dry sponge to ink inner and outer edges of cardboard frame.

Cut rippled-sand-patterned paper the same size as front of cardboard frame; cut opening for photo in the center. Use a dry sponge to ink inner and outer edges of rippled-sand frame; glue fiber ribbon down center of each side, leaving ends long enough to wrap around to back.

Use a dry sponge to ink inner and outer edges of slide mounts. Cut six mini collages from stamp-collage paper; glue one to the back of each slide mount. Center and punch a 1⁄16-inch hole at top and bottom of each slide mount; insert brads through holes. Glue slide mounts over ribbon down each side of rippled-sand frame.

Sand bookplates with sandpaper. Brush black acrylic paint over bookplates and immediately wipe off excess with a dry paper towel. Use computer or hand print "TRUE LOVE" and names on dark pink card stock to fit within rectangles that will fit in bookplates; cut out and adhere to back of bookplates.

Center bookplates on top and bottom panels of rippled-sand frame; mark holes with pencil. Punch 1⁄16-inch holes at pencil marks. Adhere bookplates to rippled-sand frame, aligning holes. Insert brads through holes.

Glue rippled-sand frame to cardboard frame. Wrap ribbon ends around to back; glue. Mount photo in frame. ■

SOURCES: Frame from All Night Media/Plaid; embossed paper from K&Company; patterned paper from The Paper Loft; brads from Creative Impressions; Zip Dry instant-dry paper glue from Beacon.

MATERIALS

- 7½ x 6-inch white cardboard frame
- Stamp-collage embossed paper
- Rippled-sand-patterned paper
- Dark pink card stock
- 13⁄16 x 1⅝-inch silver bookplates
- 6 (2-inch) slide mounts
- 5 x 3½-inch photo
- 12 pewter mini brads
- Red fiber ribbon
- Brown dye ink pad
- Black acrylic paint
- 1⁄16-inch circle punch
- Small sponge
- Sandpaper
- Paintbrush
- Paper towel
- Instant-dry paper glue
- Computer fonts (optional)

Happy
VALENTINE'S DAY
FROM YOUR GIRLS
YOU

LOVE
noun | verb
['ləv]
Ll
synonyms: affection, attachment, devotion, fondness, amour, passion, amourousness, beloved, darling, turtledove, dear, honey, loveling, sweet, adoration
see: worship, adore, like, hold dear, cherish, prize, treasure
YOU

Hidden Photo Card

Design by KATHLEEN PANEITZ

Tuck a precious photo behind the greeting of this unique card. A spinning tab holds it in place.

Form a 5⅛ x 5-inch card from beige card stock. Cut a 5⅛ x 3-inch strip of plaid patterned paper; sand edges with sandpaper and adhere to card. Ink edges of card and "Love" tab. Adhere a ¾-inch-wide strip of plaid patterned paper across back of "Love" tab, near bottom. Transfer "Happy Valentine's Day" rub-on transfers to back of "Love" tab.

Set two eyelets 1 inch apart along left front edge of "Love" tab; set matching eyelets on card front, just to left of plaid strip. Using circle punch, punch matching holes on card front ¾ inch to right of eyelets.

Use label maker to print "from your girls" on black label tape; peel backing and adhere down back of "Love" tab, ½ inch from edge with eyelets. Print "you" on label tape; peel backing and adhere to front of card, near bottom right corner.

Cut a 3-inch piece of black twill tape in half lengthwise. From inside card, thread end through eyelet in card front; thread other end through punched hole, then eyelet on "Love" tab. Knot ends on front and trim, leaving enough "play" so tab can be folded "open." Repeat with second piece of twill tape.

Trim photo to fit behind "Love" tab; adhere photo to card so that it is hidden when "Love" tab is in closed position. Use circle punch to punch hole through card front near upper right corner of photo. Mount black photo anchor over hole with black mini brad. Swing anchor over edge of "Love" tab to hold tab closed and conceal photo.

Cut a ¾-inch square of black card stock. Adhere a ¾ x 7⁄16-inch strip plaid patterned paper to square. Use circle punch to punch hole through both layers; mount heart brad through hole. Adhere square to front of "Love" tab. ■

SOURCES: Patterned paper from Deluxe Designs; tab and rub-on transfers from Autumn Leaves; distressing ink from Ranger; eyelets from The Stamp Doctor; photo anchor from Making Memories; mini brad from Magic Scraps; heart brad from Creative Impressions; label maker and tape from Dymo.

MATERIALS

- Card stock: textured beige (for card) and scrap of black
- Burgundy/pink/orange plaid patterned paper
- "Love" tab
- Burgundy word rub-on transfers
- Antique linen distressing-ink pad
- 4 silver oval eyelets with eyelet-setting tool
- Black photo anchor
- Black mini brad
- Pewter heart brad
- Label maker with ⅜-inch-wide black tape
- ⅜-inch-wide black twill tape
- 1⁄16-inch circle punch
- Black-and-white photo
- Sandpaper
- Adhesive

A measure
of my Love
For
From

Measure of Love Gift Bag

Design by BARBARA GREVE

Let your loved ones know exactly how they measure up with a gift given in this little bag embellished with tape measure and ruler papers.

MATERIALS

- 8¼ x 5⅛-inch red paper shopping bag with handles
- Red corrugated paper
- White card stock
- Tape measure patterned paper
- Love words patterned paper
- Natural raffia
- Alphabet rub-on transfers
- Acrylic square and circle stickers
- Ruler sticker
- Greetings rubber stamp
- Black ink pad
- Gloss decoupage medium
- ⅛-inch circle punch
- Paper piercer
- Large-eye needle
- Permanent adhesive

Using pattern provided, cut heart from red corrugated paper. Using paper piercer, punch holes where indicated on pattern. Thread needle with raffia; stitch up from the back through one of the outer holes and take needle down through center hole. Stitch up through next outer hole and down through center hole again; continue around pattern until complete. Knot raffia ends on back.

Using ⅛-inch circle punch, punch holes around top of bag ½ inch apart and ¼ inch from edge. Thread needle with raffia; beginning in a back corner, work overcast stitch through holes around top of bag. Knot ends together and trim.

Cut a 3-inch square of tape measure paper; center and decoupage onto front of bag 1¼ inches below top edge. Transfer alphabet rub-ons onto bag. Adhere clear acrylic circle over "m" in "measure" and clear acrylic square over "L" in "Love." Using permanent adhesive, adhere stitched heart in center of tape measure paper.

Cut a 2⅛ x 1⅝-inch tag shape from red corrugated paper. Using ⅛-inch circle punch, punch hole in top of tag. Cut a 1½ x 2-inch rectangle of love words patterned paper; using permanent adhesive, adhere love words rectangle in center of red corrugated tag. Using greetings stamp and black ink, stamp "To" and "From" onto love words rectangle.

Cut first 3½ inches off ruler sticker; adhere to white card stock and cut out. Using ⅛-inch circle punch, punch hole in end of ruler tag. String ruler tag and red corrugated tag onto raffia; tie around bag handle in a bow. ■

SOURCES: Patterned papers from 7gypsies; rub-on transfers, acrylic square and circle stickers from Making Memories; additional rub-on transfers from EK Success; ruler sticker from K&Company; Anna Griffin stamps and decoupage medium from Plaid; permanent adhesive from Beacon.

DRAWING on page 158

Happy
Valentine's
__Day

Octopus Gift Bag

Design by LORETTA MATEIK

Replace the stamped legs of this fun octopus with wiggly, giggly red wire. Shrink-plastic heart charms add dimension and motion.

Project note: *Adhere elements with double-stick adhesive tape unless otherwise instructed.*

Cut 1¾ x 2-inch and 1⁵⁄₁₆ x 1⅝-inch rectangles from white card stock. Cut 1½ x 1¹³⁄₁₆-inch and ⅞ x 1-inch rectangles from red card stock. Center and adhere larger red rectangle on larger white rectangle.

Using paper piercer, make two tiny holes ⅛ inch apart through smaller white rectangle, ½ inch from bottom edge (see drawing). Cut red wire in 7-, 6-, 5-, 4- and 1½-inch pieces. Thread 1½-inch wire from back to front through one hole in smaller white rectangle. Center and hold remaining red wires together; lay on front of pierced white card stock. Thread end of 1½-inch wire through other hole, catching bundle of wires. Twist ends of 1½-inch wire together on back to hold wires. Center and adhere card stock with wires to red/white rectangles assembled earlier.

On another piece of white card stock, stamp octopus using red ink. Cut out, cutting off legs. Bend and curl wires to form octopus legs. Using dimensional adhesive dot, adhere stamped octopus to tops of legs.

Scuff shrink plastic with sandpaper. Using red solvent ink, stamp hearts on shrink plastic. Cut out; punch a ¹⁄₁₆-inch hole in the top of each. Shrink hearts with heat tool. Wire hearts onto ends of octopus arms.

Use computer and red ink or hand print "Happy Valentine's Day" on plain white paper to fit within a ¾ x 1⁵⁄₁₆-inch rectangle; cut out and adhere to red ⅞ x 1-inch card stock rectangle. Wire onto end of one arm.

Using ¼-inch circle punch, punch a hole on each side of bag near top. Adhere hole reinforcements over holes inside and outside bag. Cut a 10-inch piece of heart-print ribbon; thread ends through holes from outside to inside. Tie a knot in each end to hold ribbon handle in place. ■

SOURCES: Stamps from Stampin' Up!; solvent ink pad from Tsukineko; wire from Artistic Wire.

DRAWING on page 158

MATERIALS

- Card stock: white and red
- 6¾ x 3 x 1⅞-inch red gift bag
- White paper
- White shrink plastic
- Rubber stamps: hearts and octopus
- Red dye ink pad
- Red solvent ink pad
- ⅜-inch-wide red-and-white heart-print ribbon
- 26-gauge red craft wire
- 4 red round hole reinforcements
- Sandpaper
- Paper cutter (optional)
- Heat tool
- ¹⁄₁₆-inch and ¼-inch circle punches
- Paper piercer
- Double-stick adhesive tape
- Dimensional adhesive dots
- Computer font (optional)

S.W.A.K. Gift Bag

Design by LORETTA MATEIK

Sparkling lips add a whimsical touch to a gift bag that's "sealed with a kiss" for valentine gift giving.

***Project note:** Adhere elements with double-stick adhesive tape unless otherwise instructed.*

Using pattern provided, cut print tag from heart-print paper, positioning pattern so as to leave two hearts extending over edge as shown. Partially release hearts that will extend over "S.W.A.K." label by cutting along dashed lines with craft knife.

Adhere "S.W.A.K." sticker to white card stock; trim to measure 1¹⁄₁₆ x 1⅞ inches. Adhere card stock with sticker to heart print tag, tucking corners and edge behind cut-away sections of hearts. Adhere heart-print tag to white card stock; trim around tag leaving a narrow white border. Punch ¹⁄₁₆-inch hole in top of tag; set eyelet in hole.

Using a sharp needle, punch four tiny holes through tag where indicated by dots at ends of scrolls on pattern. Thread wire through top hole from back to front; bend wire to form a scroll matching the scroll on the pattern, then thread wire to back through next hole. Bring wire up again in third hole; form second scroll and thread wire to back through final hole. Curl wire ends on back of tag to hold scrolls in place.

From remaining heart-print paper, cut a small and a medium heart; adhere over matching hearts on tag using pieces cut from adhesive foam dots.

Thread ⅛-inch satin ribbon through eyelet; tie tag to bag handle. Tuck white tissue into bag. Randomly adhere felt lips to tissue paper that peeks over top of bag. ■

MATERIALS

- 10 x 8-inch red paper shopping bag with handles
- Heart-print paper
- White card stock
- White tissue
- "S.W.A.K." sticker
- Pink and red felt lips with glitter
- ⅛-inch-wide white satin ribbon
- 26-gauge red wire
- White eyelet and eyelet-setting tool
- ¹⁄₁₆-inch circle punch
- Sharp needle or awl
- Craft knife
- Double-stick adhesive tape
- Adhesive foam dots

SOURCES: Patterned paper from Provo Craft; sticker from Mrs. Grossman's; felt lips from CPE; wire from Artistic Wire.

DRAWING on page 159

Always Valentine Tag

Design by SUSAN STRINGFELLOW

Embellish the front of a simple tag with wildly romantic items such as antique buttons and lace!

Cut a 4½ x 3-inch piece of green patterned paper; tear along bottom edge. Mat on green card stock, adhering with glue stick; tear along bottom edge of card stock.

Fold a small piece of vintage lace or tatted edging to resemble a handkerchief; affix butterfly pin to lace. Adhere "handkerchief" to bottom left corner with paper glaze.

Cut out valentine image; tear along bottom edge. Rub edges of valentine image on embossing ink pad; sprinkle with gold embossing powder and emboss. Mat valentine image on rose card stock, adhering with glue stick; tear rose card stock along bottom edge. Adhere rose tag to green tag at an angle with glue stick, overlapping handkerchief.

Adhere "Always" sticker in upper left corner of tag. Adhere buttons and leaf beads above lace with paper glaze. Punch hole through top of tag; cut fibers 7–9 inches long and thread through hole. ■

SOURCES: Patterned paper from Creative Imaginations; vintage image from Altered Pages; sticker from NRN Designs; beads from Blue Moon Beads; paper glaze from JudiKins.

MATERIALS

- Card stock: green and rose
- Green patterned paper
- Vintage valentine image, approximately 4 x 2 7/16 inches
- "Always" sticker
- Clear embossing ink
- Metallic gold embossing powder
- Vintage lace or tatted edging
- 2 Victorian-style buttons
- Glass leaf beads
- Gold butterfly pin
- Decorative fibers: peach, green and gold
- Paper glaze
- Embossing heat gun
- ¼-inch circle punch
- Glue stick

groink

Pig Cookie Canister

Design by MARY AYRES

Help your friends celebrate National Pig Day with a canister filled with yummy treats!

Cut corrugated paper to fit around can with ridges running vertically, piecing as needed. Rub longer edges with pink ink pad.

From remaining corrugated paper cut one snout, two nostrils, two eyes, and one ear circle, cut in half, for ears. Rub edges of all pieces with pink ink pad.

Arrange snout, nostrils, eyes and ears on larger strip of corrugated paper. Glue in place, applying glue only to center of snout and only to top inner corners of ears, as these pieces will not lie flat against can.

Punch ⅛-inch holes in top corners of ears, and in centers of eyes and nostrils. Attach pink paper fasteners in ear and nostril holes, and blue fasteners in eye holes. Glue assembled strip around sides of can.

From remaining corrugated paper, cut strips to fit around spools with ridges running vertically. Rub longer edges with pink ink pad; glue strips around spools. Glue spools to bottom of can for legs.

Cut a circle of corrugated paper to fit in center of lid; rub edges with pink ink pad and glue to lid. Place lid on can.

Wrap grosgrain ribbon around can between front and back legs; tie ends in a bow on top. Tie checked ribbon in a bow; glue below snout.

Tag: Use computer or hand print "groink" on white card stock. Trim so that lettering is positioned toward the left on a 3 x 1-inch rectangle. Punch a ⅛-inch hole in right side of tag; set eyelet in hole. Thread cord through eyelet; tie tag around bow loop on top of canister. ■

SOURCES: Instant-dry paper glue from Beacon.

DRAWINGS on page 159

MATERIALS

- New, clean, quart paint can with lid
- Beige corrugated paper
- White card stock
- Bright pink dye ink pad
- Paper fasteners: 4 bright pink, 2 bright blue
- 4 wooden spools, 1³⁄₁₆ x ⅞ inch
- White cord
- ⅝-inch-wide ribbon: pink-and-white gingham check and pink grosgrain
- ⅛-inch silver eyelet and eyelet-setting tool
- ⅛-inch circle punch
- Instant-dry paper glue
- Computer font (optional)

Pig Family Magnets

Designs by LARA GUSTAFSON

Painted papier-mâché ornaments form the base for these cute magnets that honor the tongue-in-cheek holiday of National Pig Day.

MATERIALS

- Papier-mâché ornaments: 1 small round, 1 medium oval and 2 small ovals
- Card stock: light pink and medium pink
- Pink acrylic paint
- Medium pink chalk
- Fuzzy pink fiber
- Black fine-tip permanent marker
- 3 magnet strips
- ½-inch and ¾-inch circle punches
- White tacky craft glue

Paint all ornaments pink; let dry.

Punch two ½-inch circles from light pink card stock and one ¾-inch circle from medium pink card stock. Trace around a quarter twice onto medium pink card stock; cut out. Draw four ears freehand on light pink card stock for piglets; draw two ears on medium pink card stock for mama pig. Cut out. Cut curly tails from medium pink card stock.

For piglets, glue the light pink circles to the medium pink circles for snouts. Draw eyes and nostrils with marker. Shade ears with chalk; draw details with marker and glue ears to back of head. Glue heads over left edge of small oval ornaments. Glue tail and four 1-inch pieces of fiber for legs to back of each piglet. Attach a magnet strip.

For mama pig, glue the medium pink circle to the round ornament for snout. Draw eyes and nostrils with marker. Shade ears with chalk; draw details with marker and glue ears to back of head. Glue head over left edge of large oval ornament. Glue tail and four 1-inch pieces of fiber for legs to back of pig. Attach a magnet strip. ■

SOURCES: Circle punches from Uchida of America.

Pink Pig CD

Design by SUSAN HUBER

Choose your favorite pig-print paper and display it proudly on the face of this altered CD.

Project note: *Adhere elements with clear-drying glue unless otherwise instructed.*

Thoroughly sand front and back surfaces of CD with sandpaper so that glue will adhere. Lay CD over heavyweight mulberry paper; trace around CD and cut out. Adhere heavyweight mulberry paper to CD. Tear a 2-inch-wide strip of pig print paper; adhere diagonally across CD. Trim edges. Adhere multicolored fringe along edges of pig print paper.

Unwrap pink twisted paper; wrap it around slide mount to cover. Adhere a square of pink card stock behind slide mount; write "PIG" in center with black fine-tip marker. Wrap multicolored fringe around corners of slide mount; adhere slide mount to CD.

Cut pig outline from light pink card stock and pig front (with legs) and snout from medium pink card stock using pig die cutter. Mount medium pink pieces on light pink outline using tiny pieces of foam tape. Add eyes and nostrils using black fine-tip marker. Adhere entire pig to CD, overlapping slide mount, using foam tape.

Glue fuzzy pink cord around edge of CD. Attach a piece of fuzzy pink fringe through pig's curly tail. ■

SOURCES: Twisted paper from Making Memories; slide mount from Magic Scraps; pig die cut from QuicKutz.

MATERIALS

- Blank CD
- Card stock: textured light pink and textured medium pink
- Pink heavyweight mulberry paper
- Patterned paper with pig and farm designs
- Variegated pink twisted paper
- Slide mount
- Decorative pink and multicolored fibers
- Black fine-tip marker
- Sandpaper
- Craft knife
- Pig die cut
- Foam tape
- Clear-drying glue

KISS ME!
I'M IRISH!

Kiss Me, I'm Irish! Frame

Design by SANDY ROLLINGER

Frame a kissable face with a time-honored Irish saying and a bit of traditional quilling.

Project notes: *Glue ends of quilled paper strips with paper glue to secure individual shapes.*
Refer to photo for placement of quilled shapes.
Use instant-dry glue unless otherwise instructed.

Paint front and back of frame with two coats gold paint, letting it dry between coats.

Use paper trimmer to cut two 1 x 5½-inch strips and two 1 x 7-inch strips of white card stock. Run strips through crimper and glue to frame.

Cut 14 (7-inch) strips of green quilling paper. Roll each strip into a teardrop. Flatten the large end of two teardrops to form stems. Using paper glue, glue the remaining teardrops together in pairs to form hearts. Set aside.

Cut two 6-inch pieces of wire. Curl one end into a spiral. String gold and white beads on wires, forming loops after every few beads. Form curls in the last inch of each wire. Glue wires to frame.

Use the paper trimmer to cut four 1½-inch squares of medium green card stock; trim edges with decorative scissors. Glue squares to corners of frame.

Glue three quilled hearts to bottom left square to form a shamrock; add quilled stem. Repeat in top right corner.

Use computer or hand print "KISS ME!" and "I'M IRISH" on light green card stock, using a bold font that will fit on frame. Trim around phrases with decorative-edge scissors; glue to frame.

Sew floss through buttonholes; knot on back. Glue buttons around phrases. ■

SOURCES: Metallic paint from Jacquard Products; instant-dry paper glue and paper glue from Beacon.

DRAWINGS on page 160

MATERIALS

- 6 x 7½ wooden frame
- Metallic gold acrylic paint
- Card stock: light green, medium green and white
- Green ⅛-inch-wide paper quilling strips
- 26-gauge gold wire
- 5mm gold beads
- White seed beads
- Assorted green buttons: hearts, medium and small rounds
- Gold embroidery floss and needle
- ¾ oval wash paintbrush
- Paper crimper
- Decorative-edge scissors
- Slotted quilling tool
- Wire cutter
- Computer font (optional)
- Instant-dry paper glue
- Paper glue

luck

Luck 'o The Irish Mini Album

Design by BARBARA GREVE

Simple embroidered stitches form a lucky four-leaf clover to embellish the front of a tiny journal!

MATERIALS

- Ivy-print reversible card stock
- Tan corrugated paper
- 4 sheets plain white paper
- Scrap of white vellum
- 2 light green frame fasteners
- 2 light green square stud fasteners
- 1 x 2-inch rectangular vellum tag
- 10 (⅛-inch) silver eyelets and eyelet-setting tool
- Black alphabet rub-on transfers
- Green paper raffia
- Green jute
- Tracing paper
- Paper piercer
- Large-eye sewing needle
- ⅛-inch circle punch
- Permanent adhesive
- Instant-dry paper glue

Cut a 2¾ x 2⅜-inch rectangle of tan corrugated paper with grooves running horizontally with shorter sides of rectangle. Using pattern provided, trace shamrock onto tracing paper; center traced pattern on corrugated rectangle. Using paper piercer, make holes where indicated on pattern. Thread needle with raffia; fill in the clover leaves and stem with satin stitches. Knot raffia ends on back.

Cut two 6-inch squares of reversible card stock for covers. Position stitched rectangle on front cover 2¼ inches in from left edge and above bottom edge; adhere with permanent adhesive.

Punch two holes through front cover at each corner of stitched rectangle; punch two more holes 1½ inches below stitched rectangle and 1¼ inches apart for attaching vellum tag. Punch matching holes in vellum tag. Transfer "luck" rub-ons to vellum tag; mount tag on cover with silver eyelets. Set eyelets in remaining holes. Thread green jute through corner eyelets across corners of stitched rectangle; tie off on back.

Cut a 6 x 2⅛-inch strip of tan corrugated paper with grooves running lengthwise for album spine. Adhere edges of front and back covers to wrong side of spine with permanent adhesive, leaving 3⁄16 inch between edges of covers. Fold album closed with cover edges even; punch holes through all layers 1 inch from top and bottom and ¼ inch to left of spine's inner edge. Punch three more holes between them, spacing holes 1 inch apart.

Cut eight 5½-inch squares of plain white paper for pages. Stack pages with edges even; insert inside cover with left edges against spine; mark through holes with a pencil. Remove pages; punch holes at pencil marks.

Insert pages in cover, aligning holes. Thread large-eye needle with green raffia. Sew through top hole from back to front, leaving a 10-inch raffia tail. Sew album together with a running stitch from top to bottom and back up to top. Bring raffia tail over top; tie raffia ends in a bow on front.

Cut two ⅝-inch triangles of white vellum; adhere in outer corners of front cover with instant-dry paper glue. Set stud fasteners in vellum corners. Set frame fasteners in opposite corners. ■

SOURCES: Double-sided card stock from Bo-Bunny Press; fasteners from Scrapworks; vellum tag, eyelets and rub-on transfers from Making Memories; permanent adhesive and instant-dry paper glue from Beacon; paper raffia from DMD Inc.

DRAWING on page 160

Shamrock Pins

Designs by SANDY ROLLINGER

Don't get pinched for not wearing green this St. Paddy's Day. Wear one of these easy-to-create pins!

Use brush to dust candy mold with cornstarch. Press a 1-inch ball of modeling compound into the mold; pop out and trim excess clay with scissors. Smooth edges with fingers. Repeat to make a second shamrock; let dry overnight.

Paint shamrocks with two coats green paint; dry after each coat.

Randomly brush gold ink from ink pad over one shamrock. Sprinkle with gold embossing powder; tap off excess and emboss. Clip shank off button with wire cutters; glue to center of shamrock.

Randomly brush clear embossing ink from ink pad over second shamrock. Sprinkle with holographic embossing powder; tap off excess and emboss. Glue rhinestones to center in a shamrock shape.

Glue pin backs to shamrocks; let dry overnight. ■

SOURCES: Air-dry modeling compound from Creative Paperclay Co. Inc.; paint from Jacquard Products; craft cement from Beacon.

MATERIALS

- Blue air-dry modeling compound
- 2-inch shamrock candy mold
- Pearl emerald green acrylic paint
- Metallic gold ink pad
- Clear embossing ink pad
- Embossing powder: gold and holographic
- Small gold shank button
- 3 small flat crystal rhinestone hearts
- Cornstarch
- 2 (1-inch) pin backs
- Heat embossing tool
- Soft, flat paintbrush
- Wire cutters
- Craft scissors
- Craft cement

St. Patrick's Day Candy Box

Design by LORETTA MATEIK

Collect the gold from the end of the rainbow and tuck it inside this tiny gift box!

Leaving rainbow sticker intact, apply paper glaze in a thin stripe along right edge of sticker. Sprinkle glaze with red glitter; tap off excess. Repeat to apply paper glaze and stripes of green, blue and yellow glitter to sticker. ***Note:*** *Though there is no green stripe on the sticker, green glitter will add color to the rainbow.*

Using the pattern provided, cut one pot from black card stock. Cut a 1⅚₁₆ x 1⁵⁄₁₆-inch rectangle from green card stock. Use computer and green ink or hand print "Happy St. Patrick's Day" on plain white paper to fit within a ¾ x 1¹⁄₁₆-inch rectangle; cut out and adhere to green card stock rectangle using double-stick tape.

Using ¹⁄₁₆-inch circle punch, punch a hole on each side of box, ¼ inch from top. For handle, thread ends of a 10-inch piece of fine rat-tail cord through holes from outside to inside. Tie a knot in each end to hold cord handle in place.

Trim clouds off rainbow sticker. Using double-sided tape, adhere rainbow sticker to front of box. Using dimensional adhesive dots, adhere pot in bottom right corner and sign in upper right corner. Fill box with foil-wrapped chocolate coins. ■

SOURCES: Park Borders rainbow sticker from Me & My Big Ideas; paper glaze from JudiKins.

DRAWING on page 160

MATERIALS

- Card stock: black and green
- Candy-bar box with window
- Rainbow sticker
- Fine glitter: red, blue, green and yellow
- Green satin fine rat-tail cord
- Gold-foil-covered chocolate coins
- Paper glaze
- ¹⁄₁₆-inch circle punch
- Double-stick tape
- Dimensional adhesive dots
- Computer font (optional)

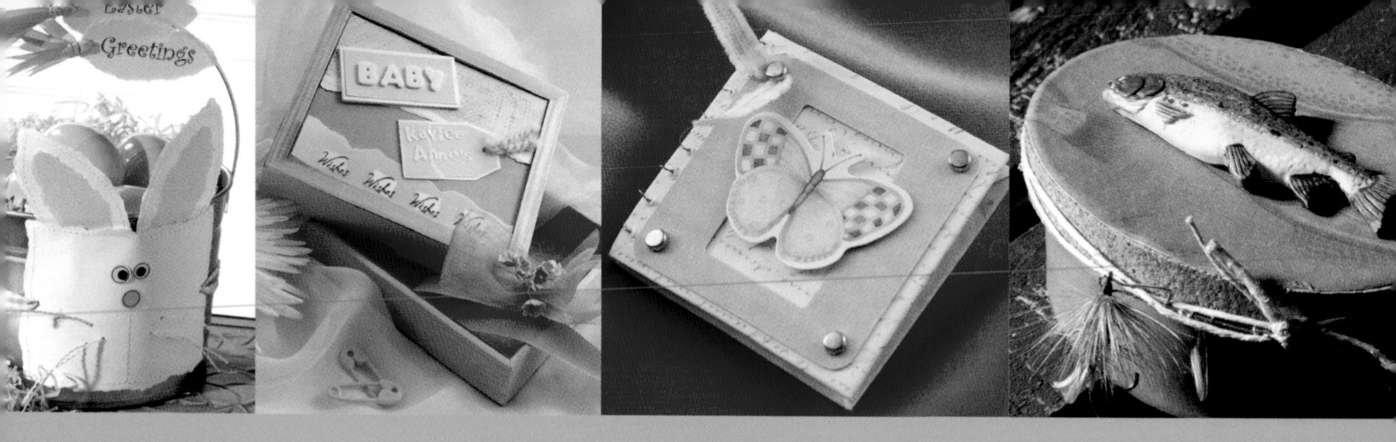

April Through June

Spring cheer abounds as the gray days of winter turn sunny and bright. Create a fun gift that reflects the warmth and color of the season!

Key to my heart
Michael Paul Rojas

Easter
Greetings

Easter Greetings Bucket

Design by MARY AYRES

Colorful surprise-filled plastic eggs and other tiny treats are wonderful additions to this bucket embellished with a sweet bunny.

MATERIALS

- 7½ x 5-inch unused metal paint can
- Card stock: white, light pink, dark pink, black and orange
- 4 (⅛-inch) round silver eyelets and eyelet-setting tool
- 1 yard ⅝-inch-wide purple-and-white checked ribbon
- 1⅓ yards ⅜-inch-wide green satin ribbon
- Strands pulled from off-white burlap
- Black fine-tip permanent marker
- Punches: 1⁄16-, ⅛-, ¼- and ½-inch circle punches
- Sewing machine and off-white all-purpose thread
- Hot-glue gun with glue stick
- Instant-dry paper glue
- Computer font (optional)

Project note: *Unused metal paint cans are available at most home-improvement stores.*

Tear a 4 x 5-inch rectangle from white card stock for head; tear two 4 x 2-inch teardrop shapes from white card stock for ears. Tear two 3½ x 1½-inch teardrop shapes from light pink card stock for inner ears. Center and adhere pink inner ears in white ears using instant-dry paper glue.

Referring to pattern provided, begin at top of muzzle, under nose area, and machine stitch down center of head, then continue stitching around head in a continuous line. Machine stitch around ears. Glue ears to back of head.

Using 1⁄16-inch punch, punch six holes in head for whisker dots. Thread a 3-inch strand of burlap through each hole; knot on wrong side. Using ½-inch punch, punch one circle from dark pink card stock for nose and two circles from light pink card stock for eyes. Using fine-tip black marker, outline eye and nose circles close to edge. Using ¼-inch punch, punch two circles from black card stock for pupils. Using instant-dry paper glue, adhere pupils to eyes; adhere nose and eyes to bunny.

Using ⅛-inch punch, center and punch a hole on each side of head, near edge. Set eyelets in holes. Cut checked ribbon in half; thread one piece through *both* eyelets across back of head, with ends extending on front. Lay remaining purple checked ribbon around back of bucket; position bunny head at front of bucket and knot ribbons at the sides. Notch ribbon ends.

For carrots, use computer or hand print "Easter Greetings" on orange card stock, leaving space between the words. Tear around words so that each is centered in a 3 x 1⅛-inch teardrop-shaped carrot. Using ⅛-inch punch, punch a hole in broad end of each carrot. Set eyelets in holes. Using instant-dry paper glue, adhere carrots to each other so that they overlap.

For carrot greens, cut green ribbon into six 8-inch pieces. Hold two pieces together with ends even and thread halfway through eyelet in "Greetings" carrot; hold all four ends together. Wrap base of greens with a third piece of ribbon; knot on back. Repeat with "Easter" carrot, tying carrots to bucket handle with ribbon used to wrap greens. Notch ribbon ends. Using hot-glue gun, adhere "Easter" carrot to bucket handle. ■

SOURCE: Adhesive from Beacon.

DRAWINGS on page 161

Easter Egg Gift Set

Designs by BARBARA GREVE

Nestle a tiny gift in this darling basket and add a personal greeting on the coordinating egg-shaped album.

EASTER BASKET

Cut 16–20 12 x ½-inch-wide strips each from solid pink and pink checked papers, enough to cover cardboard box when woven.

Turn box upside down. Lay pink checked strips side by side and lengthwise across box bottom so that they will extend beyond top of box when folded over short ends. Hold strips in place with straight pins; cover bottom of box completely. Weave solid pink strips through pink checked strips, making sure that they will extend beyond top of box when folded over long sides.

DRAWINGS on page 162

MATERIALS

- Small cardboard box, approximately 3 x 4 x 2¾ inches
- Patterned papers: pink check, solid white and solid pink
- Yellow corrugated paper
- Crinkled pink paper shreds
- 4 (⅛-inch) yellow eyelets and eyelet-setting tool
- Raffia: pink, green and yellow
- 28-gauge craft wire: 26 inches each pink and yellow
- Fine white cotton string
- 14 inches fine yellow craft cord
- Straight pins
- 4 x 3-inch and 3½ x 2½-inch oval templates with cutter
- Rotary cutter with mat (optional)
- ⅛-inch circle punch
- Paper piercer
- Large-eye needle
- Wire cutters
- Instant-dry paper glue
- Permanent adhesive

Bunny Trail Gift Box

Design by SUSAN STRINGFELLOW

Brightly colored ribbon streamers close the top of this cheerful Easter gift box. Because it's quick to create, you'll want to make several to give to all your favorite kids!

For front and back of box, cut two 6½ x 3¼-inch rectangles from striped card stock; trim top corners to create tag shapes. Cut two ¾-inch squares of solid orange card stock; mat each on solid green card stock. Center and adhere one orange/green square at top edge of each tag with permanent adhesive. Punch hole through all layers with ¼-inch circle punch.

Stamp bunny border on box with embossing ink; apply white embossing powder and emboss. Stamp words with black ink.

Paint metal flower tile in assorted sherbet colors. When dry, sand surface lightly. Punch a hole in flower center with a nail. Insert pink flower brad through hole; attach metal flower tile to box.

For sides and bottom of gift box, cut a strip of pink patterned card stock 11¾ x 2¾ inches. Score two lines down length of strip, ¼ inch from each long edge. Score across width of strip 4¼ inches from each end, where sides will fold up; cut notches in the ¼-inch allowance at each of these folds. Apply permanent adhesive to ¼-inch tabs on pink patterned card stock strip; adhere strip between front and back of box.

Cut four 16-inch lengths of assorted ribbons; tie through holes in top of box. ■

SOURCES: Patterned card stock from SEI; PSX stamp from Duncan; word stamps from Hero Arts; solvent ink pad from Tsukineko; tile from ScrapYard; acrylic paints and brad from Making Memories.

MATERIALS

- Card stocks in coordinating "sherbet" colors: striped, solid orange, solid green and pink patterned
- Bunny border rubber stamp
- Word rubber stamps
- Black solvent ink pad
- Clear embossing ink
- White embossing powder
- Embossed metal flower tile
- Acrylic paints in assorted "sherbet" colors
- Pink flower brad
- Decorative ribbons
- Paintbrush
- ¼-inch circle punch
- Embossing heat tool
- Rotary cutter with scoring tool (optional)
- Sandpaper
- Nail
- Permanent adhesive

Shades of Spring Baby Set

Designs by SANDY ROLLINGER

Delight a new mom with this adorable duo created in pretty yellows and blues. Attach a gift card to the end of the gift box streamer as a surprise gift!

BUNNIES, DUCKS & BUTTONS

Use brayer to roll yellow modeling compound ⅛ inch thick on glass surface. Use cookie cutter to cut two ducks from modeling compound; use clay cutter to cut two teardrops for wings. Use brayer to roll white modeling compound ⅛ inch thick on glass surface. Use cookie cutter to cut three bunnies from modeling compound. Let pieces dry overnight.

Dot bunnies with pink opaque paper paint; dot ducks and wings with metallic white pearl paint. Let dry. Adhere wings to ducks using instant-dry paper glue.

Thread needle with white embroidery floss. Thread floss through holes in flat pastel buttons. Knot ends on front of buttons; trim floss ends to ¼ inch.

FRAME

Spray frame with gesso; let dry. Using paintbrush, paint frame yellow; let dry. Add a second coat of yellow paint. Dab small sponge onto gold ink pad, then dab sponge randomly on frame. Let dry. Dot frame with metallic white pearl paint. Let dry.

Cut two strips of vellum ½ x 4¼ inches and two strips ½ x 6 inches; run strips through crimper. Use dots of instant-dry paper glue to adhere strips around frame opening. Use permanent adhesive to adhere rickrack around outer edge of frame.

Use instant-dry paper glue to adhere one duck in upper left corner and one bunny in lower right corner. Use wire cutters to snap shanks off baby theme buttons. Adhere baby theme buttons and pastel buttons around frame.

BOX

Spray box and lid, inside and outside, with gesso; let dry. Using paintbrush, paint box and lid, inside and out, with yellow paint; let dry, then add a second coat of yellow paint. Dab small sponge onto gold ink pad, then dab sponge randomly over box and lid. Let dry. Dot box and lid with metallic white pearl paint. Let dry.

Cut one strip of light blue card stock ½ x 12½ inches; run strip through crimper. Use dots of instant-dry paper glue to adhere strip around edge of lid. Use permanent adhesive to adhere rickrack around lid, over crimped card stock.

Use fine-tip pen to write "Welcome Baby" in a 1 x 1¼-inch rectangle of vellum; trim edges with decorative-edge scissors. Use instant-dry paper glue to glue vellum tag at one end of organza ribbon. Using permanent adhesive, glue pastel green button to ribbon next to vellum tag; adhere bunny, pink button, duck, blue button and another bunny to ribbon, spacing them evenly. Fold over other end of ribbon; adhere inside lid, in center. Adhere pastel buttons to top of lid. ■

SOURCES: Air-dry modeling compound from Creative Paperclay; paper paints from Plaid; ink pad from Jacquard; adhesives from Beacon.

MATERIALS

- 3-inch-square papier-mâché box with lid
- 8 x 6-inch wooden frame
- Air-drying modeling compound: white and yellow
- Clear vellum
- Light blue card stock
- Flat buttons in pastel green, pink and blue
- Pastel baby-theme decorative buttons
- Medium blue rickrack
- 10 inches (½-inch-wide) white organza ribbon
- Opaque paper paints: pink and metallic white pearl
- Metallic gold two-tone ink pad
- Gesso spray
- Yellow acrylic craft paint
- Tiny cookie cutters: 1½ x 1¼-inch bunny and 1½ x 1½-inch duck
- ½-inch teardrop clay cutter
- Black fine-tip permanent pen
- ½-inch-wide flat paintbrush
- Sponge
- Embroidery needle and white floss
- Wire cutters
- Paper trimmer (optional)
- Decorative-edge scissors
- Paper crimper
- Acrylic brayer
- Glass cutting surface
- Permanent adhesive
- Instant-dry paper glue

Baby's Wish Box

Design by JEN ESKRIDGE

Keep special wishes and keepsakes for a new baby close at hand in this special memory box.

***Project notes:** A 4⅝ x 5½ x 1½-inch wooden box with a lid with a recessed top was used to make the sample project. A papier-mâché box with lid may be substituted. Adhere elements with craft glue unless instructed otherwise.*

Remove existing logos or embellishments from box. Measure and cut light pink card stock to line inside of lid; adhere. Measure and cut dark pink card stock to line inside of box; adhere. Measure and cut patterned vellum to fit in bottom of box; adhere with spray adhesive.

Measure and cut light pink card stock to cover outside edges of lid; adhere. Measure and cut dark pink card stock to fit on top of lid; adhere. Use computer or hand print "Wishes" across strip of plain vellum long enough to fit across lid. Trim side and bottom edges with scissors; tear across top edge. Cut a white card stock rectangle to fit behind each word on vellum; adhere rectangles along bottom of dark pink card stock. Adhere printed vellum to dark pink card stock over rectangles using spray adhesive.

Measure and cut light pink card stock to fit across top half of lid; lay on scrap paper. Lay mesh over light pink card stock; stamp over surface using cosmetic sponge and pink ink. Remove mesh; let dry. Tear across bottom edge of stamped card stock; adhere card stock across top of lid top.

Cut a 1⅛ x 2⅜-inch rectangle of light pink card stock. Adhere it to white card stock; trim, leaving a narrow white border. Adhere card stock to white craft foam rectangle cut just slightly smaller than white card stock rectangle. Spell "BABY" on pink card stock with foam letter stickers.

Cut a 2 x 1³⁄₁₆-inch tag shape from light pink card stock. Adhere to white card stock; trim, leaving a narrow white border. Punch a hole in the tapered end of tag; thread fibers through hole. Tear a ¾ x 2-inch strip of plain vellum; wrap around square end of tag, folding edges to back; adhere using spray adhesive. Spell baby's name on tag using white paper letter stickers.

Adhere "BABY" and name tags to box lid; trim fibers and adhere to lid. ■

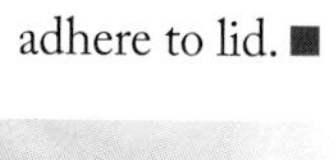

MATERIALS

Box with lid
Card stock: dark pink, light pink and white
Pink patterned vellum
Plain white vellum
Pink fibers
White craft foam
½-inch white foam letter stickers
⅜-inch white paper letter stickers
Pink ink pad
Makeup sponge or dauber
Mesh or window screen
Craft glue
Spray adhesive
Computer font (optional)

Baby Boy Frame

Design by BETH CLARK, COURTESY OF DUNCAN

Surround baby's cherished first photo with a tiny frame embellished with adorable paper.

MATERIALS

- Patterned papers: baby boy print and blue stripe
- White vellum
- Mat board
- Word rub-on transfers
- Clear acetate
- 2¼ x 1¹¹⁄₁₆-inch baby photo
- 1½-inch white tassel
- 1-inch-wide white satin ribbon
- 2 white eyelets and eyelet-setting tool
- ⅛-inch circle punch
- Sewing needle and white thread
- Glue stick
- Craft glue
- Diamond glitter glue

Cut 5 x 3-inch pointed "banner" from mat board. Adhere banner to wrong side of baby boy patterned paper using glue stick; trim around banner leaving ½-inch paper border. Fold paper to back of banner, clipping corners; adhere with glue stick. Attach tassel at bottom point using craft glue. Cut baby boy patterned paper to cover back of banner; adhere using glue stick.

Cut a 3½ x 2¼-inch piece of blue striped paper with stripes running vertically; tear top and bottom edges to make a piece 2¾ x 2¼ inches. Apply glitter glue to torn edges; let dry. Center a 2½ x 2-inch piece of acetate on striped paper; create pocket for photo by stitching acetate to paper down sides and across bottom using needle and thread. Slide photo in pocket; center and adhere striped paper to banner using glue stick.

Adhere rub-on word transfer to white vellum; trim close, then adhere vellum to banner under photo using glue stick. Punch holes in top corners of banner; apply a drop of glue in each and set eyelets in holes. Dot banner with glitter glue. Let dry. Thread ribbon through eyelets; tie in a bow. ■

SOURCES: Rub-on transfers, adhesives, glitter glue, PSX patterned paper and vellum from Duncan.

Spring Surprise Containers

Designs by MARY AYRES

Pretty enough for springtime decor, these tiny containers also hold candy or small gifts. The surprise ingredient? Recycled cardboard tubes!

MATERIALS

- Card stock: white and pastel shades of purple, green, yellow and pink
- Mulberry paper: yellow, green and orange
- 2 recycled cardboard tubes from bathroom tissue
- 2 (2½- to 3-inch) peach butterfly stickers
- 2 (⅛-inch) silver eyelets and eyelet-setting tool
- 22-gauge craft wire: purple and pink
- Metallic white craft cord
- ⅛-inch circle punch
- Assorted decorative-edge scissors
- Instant-dry paper glue
- Computer font (optional)

PURPLE, GREEN & YELLOW CONTAINER

Cover cardboard tube with purple card stock; adhere with instant-dry paper glue. Using a different decorative-edge scissors for each color, cut two 4-inch circles from green mulberry paper and two 3½-inch circles from yellow mulberry paper. Center one yellow circle on one green circle; center both over end of tube. Knot white craft cord around paper circles and tube about ⅜ inch from end, holding paper circles in place. Fill container. Cover other end with remaining mulberry paper circles secured with white craft cord.

Adhere a butterfly sticker to green card stock; trim around edge with decorative-edge scissors. Bend wings up slightly. Bend a 4-inch piece of purple wire in half; coil ends for antennae. Glue antennae to back of butterfly using instant-dry paper glue. Glue butterfly to tube at an angle.

Use computer or hand print spring sentiment on white card stock to fit in a rectangle approximately ¾ x 3 inches. Trim around words, leaving room for eyelet on left side. Punch ⅛-inch hole in left side of tag; set eyelet in hole. Thread a 2-inch piece of purple wire through eyelet and under craft cord at top of container; twist wire ends together.

PINK, GREEN & ORANGE CONTAINER

Follow basic instructions for purple, green and yellow container using materials as follows: Cover tube with pink card stock. Cut circles from green and orange mulberry paper. Adhere butterfly sticker to yellow card stock. Use pink wire. ■

SOURCES: Stickers from K&Company; wire from AMACO; adhesive from Beacon.

Butterfly Mini Notebook

Design by SUSAN HUBER

Jot down brief notes and keep them close at hand with this teeny-tiny notebook.

Center and adhere patterned paper to card stock squares using paper glue. Fold edges of paper over and adhere on back of card stock, trimming and mitering corners.

Punch seven or eight evenly spaced holes down left edge of front cover using paper piercer. Lay front cover atop back cover; punch matching holes in back cover.

Center slide mount on front cover; adhere with a mini brad in each corner. Wrap a piece of decorative fiber around brad in upper left corner. Center and adhere butterfly to front cover using foam tape.

Adhere squares of decorative paper inside covers using paper glue. Split pad of self-adhesive notes; center and adhere one section inside each cover.

Close notebook. Holding covers together, thread end of wire through holes at top and weave it in and out of holes in a spiral. Do not pull wire too tight, or book won't open and close properly. When spiral binding is complete, fold tiny loops in ends of wire. ■

SOURCES: Patterned paper from 7gypsies.

MATERIALS

- 2 (2¼-inch) squares card stock
- 2 (2¾-inch) squares cream script patterned paper
- 2-inch tan slide mount
- 4 mini brads
- Decorative fibers
- Butterfly punch-out
- Craft wire
- 2-inch pad of self-adhesive notes
- Paper piercer
- Wire cutters
- Foam tape
- Paper glue

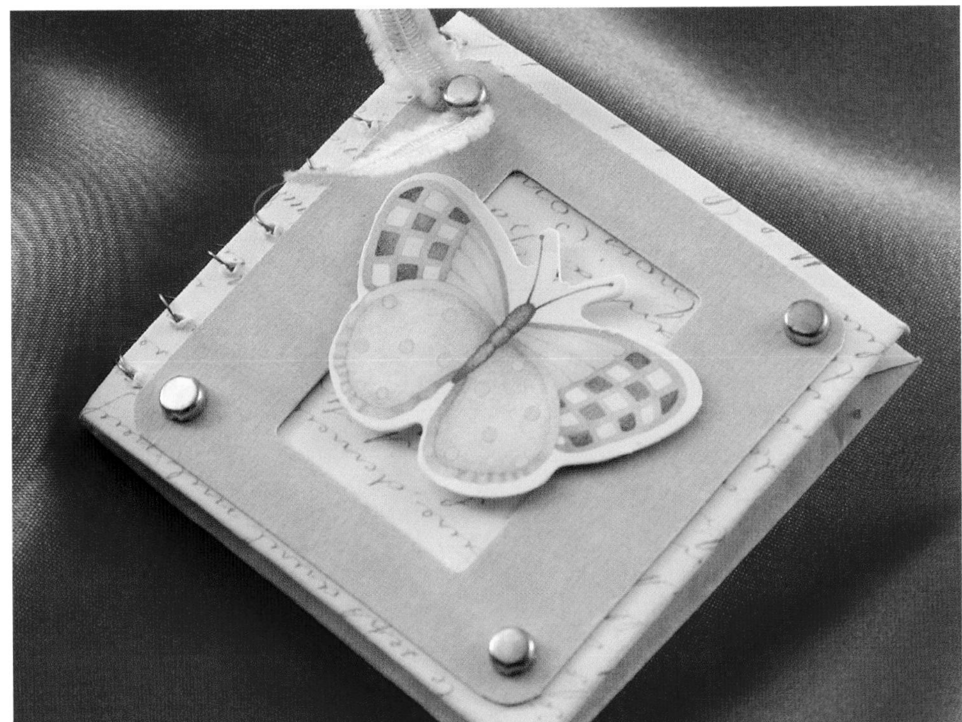

Hugs!

Framed Cat Hugs

Design by SUSAN HUBER

Cat lovers will embrace this whimsical framed wall decor featuring a stamped and painted kitty.

Stamp cat image twice on black card stock using black pigment ink; sprinkle with black embossing powder and emboss.

Mix powdered pigments to make watercolors. Paint both cat images; let dry.

Cut out select portions from one cat image, such as the bow, fish, stripes and tail. Gently curl pieces over the back of a spoon. Adhere cutout pieces over matching areas of complete cat image using pieces of foam tape cut to size. Coat cut pieces with paper glaze; let dry.

Insert wire through cat's mouth to form fishhook; twist in place. Mat cat image on 7 x 5-inch piece metallic gray paper.

FRAME

Randomly apply black pigment ink to 7 x 5-inch piece of white card stock; apply powdered pigments using dry brush. Apply more ink; sprinkle with copper embossing powder and emboss.

Cut window in embossed paper to frame cat image; cut strips for corner accents from center piece. Cut a slightly larger window in a 7 x 5-inch piece of black foam-core board.

Center and adhere matted cat image on 7 x 5-inch piece of white foam-core board using double-sided tape. Top with black foam-core frame, then embossed frame piece, adhering layers with double-sided tape. Adhere corner accents to metallic gray paper. Top framed design with acrylic panel. Break off four sections of three or four staples each; positioning staples near corners, push them into side of frame and over acrylic panel to hold layers together.

Cover foam-core edges of frame with double-sided tape. Peel off backing and coat with mixed green and gold microbeads until sides of frame are covered. Wrap fibers around frame; tie in a bow.

Stamp "Hugs!" on tag; sprinkle with gold embossing powder and emboss. Tie tag to upper left corner of frame with fibers.

Adhere a 7 x 5-inch piece of card stock on back of piece, then a cardboard frame easel, using double-sided tape. ■

SOURCES: Metal-edge tag from Making Memories; rubber stamps from Inkadinkado and Hero Arts; pigment powders from Jacquard; wire from Artistic Wire.

MATERIALS

- Card stock: black and white
- Metallic gray decorative paper
- Foam-core board: black and white
- 7 x 5 x 3/32-inch acrylic panel
- 7 x 5-inch cardboard easel back for frame
- 1 x 2-inch green rectangular metal-edge tag
- Rubber stamps: cat and "Hugs!"
- Powdered pigments in desired colors for cat and bow
- Embossing powders: copper, black and gold
- Black pigment ink pad
- Fine gold craft wire
- Green/copper decorative fibers
- Microbeads: green and gold
- Double-sided tape
- Foam tape
- Paintbrushes
- Large staples
- Embossing heat tool
- Craft knife
- Spoon
- Paper glaze

Playful Pet Trios

Designs by SANDY ROLLINGER

Wouldn't your best friend love to know you appreciate the way she feels about her pets? Show her by giving *them* a gift in these cat- or dog-themed gift sets!

Puppy Trio

CANISTER

Using acrylic roller, roll yellow modeling compound ⅛ inch thick on cutting surface. Using cookie cutter, cut one dog from modeling compound; smooth ragged edges with your finger. Lay dog over side of canister to dry overnight.

Remove dog from canister; using ½-inch brush, paint dog with two coats metallic copper paint, letting paint dry between coats. Spray with clear gloss finish; let dry.

Using black opaque paper paint, dot on eye; add nose, ear, spot on tip of tail, and toes. Using yellow-orange opaque paper paint, add collar. Let dry.

If canister lid is plastic, scuff it with sandpaper and clean with rubbing alcohol; let dry. Using a small piece of sponge, dab two coats of metallic copper paint onto lid, letting paint dry between coats. Coat with clear gloss finish; let dry.

Cut a 5-inch-wide strip of burnt orange card stock long enough to fit around canister plus 1 inch. Run strip through crimper; adhere strip to canister using instant-dry paper glue. Glue paper ends where they overlap. Let dry for 2 minutes or so, until glue holds.

Cut a 3-inch-wide strip of dark green card stock long enough to fit around canister plus 1 inch. Using two-tone ink pad, stamp paw prints on strip; let dry for about 10 seconds, then adhere around canister in center of crimped strip using instant-dry paper glue. Glue paper ends where they overlap.

Using permanent adhesive, adhere decorative fiber along edges of dark green strip; glue dog and buttons to canister.

CARD

Follow instructions for canister to roll, cut and paint one dog, but let dog lie flat to dry.

Run a 6 x 4-inch rectangle of burnt orange card stock through the paper crimper; center and adhere it to front of card using paper glue.

Randomly stamp paw prints on a 5 x 2½-inch strip of dark green card stock using two-tone ink pad. Adhere card stock to front of card at an angle using paper glue. Adhere decorative fiber around edge of dark green card stock using permanent adhesive and twisting fiber unevenly as you adhere it.

Use decorative-edge scissors to cut two rectangles of dark green card stock approximately 1½ x 2 inches; stamp with "Woof" and bone using two-tone ink pad. Let dry, then adhere to card in upper right and lower left corners using paper glue.

Glue buttons and dog to front of card using instant-dry paper glue.

MAGNET

Follow instructions for canister to roll, cut and paint one dog, but let dog lie flat to dry. Trace around finished dog on paper backing of adhesive-backed magnet sheet; cut out, cutting magnet dog slightly smaller than clay dog. Peel off paper backing and press clay dog onto magnetic shape. ■

SOURCES: Air-dry modeling compound from Creative Paperclay; metallic paint and ink pad from Jacquard; paper paints from Plaid; adhesives from Beacon.

MATERIALS

- Yellow air-drying modeling compound
- 5 x 7-inch white card with envelope
- Card stock: burnt orange and dark green
- 5-inch-tall round glass canister with lid
- Rubber stamps: "Woof," "Woof" with bone, and paw print
- Metallic copper paint
- Opaque paper paints: yellow-orange and black
- Gold/red two-tone ink pad
- Clear gloss finish
- Yellow/orange fibers
- Tan flat buttons
- Adhesive-backed magnet sheet
- 3-inch dog cookie cutter
- ½-inch paintbrush
- Paper crimper
- Paper trimmer (optional)
- Decorative-edge scissors
- Sandpaper (optional)
- Rubbing alcohol
- Acrylic roller
- Smooth cutting surface
- Household sponge
- Instant-dry paper glue
- Paper glue
- Permanent adhesive

Kitty Trio

MATERIALS

White air-drying modeling compound
5 x 7-inch white card with envelope
Purple decorative paper
Silver handmade paper
White vellum
6 x 4-inch square glass canister with metal lid
Rubber stamps: "Meow" and fish
Pearlescent violet paint
Lavender and purple flat buttons
Silver heart-shaped confetti
Adhesive-backed magnet sheet
2 x 3-inch cat cookie cutter
½-inch paintbrush
Paper crimper
Paper trimmer (optional)
Decorative-edge scissors
Acrylic roller
Smooth cutting surface
Instant-dry paper glue
Paper glue

CANISTER

Using acrylic roller, roll white modeling compound ⅛ inch thick on cutting surface. Using cookie cutter, cut four cats from modeling compound; smooth ragged edges with your finger. Lay cats flat to dry overnight.

Using ½-inch brush, paint cats with two coats of violet paint, letting paint dry between coats. Using instant-dry paper glue, glue a confetti heart to the neck of each cat.

***Note:** The following instructions are given for finishing one side of the canister; repeat to finish all sides. Work on one side of the canister at a time, letting it lay flat to dry for at least 30 minutes before working on next side.*

Tear a 4½ x 4-inch rectangle of purple paper and run it through the crimper. Center and adhere it to side of canister using instant-dry paper glue.

Cut or tear a 3 x 2-inch rectangle of silver handmade paper. Adhere it to the purple crimped paper at an angle using instant-dry paper glue.

Using decorative-edge scissors, cut a 1½ x 2¼-inch rectangle from vellum. Brush violet paint onto "Meow" with fish stamp and stamp image onto vellum; let dry. Adhere at an angle to upper right corner using paper glue.

Using instant-dry paper glue, adhere cat and buttons to canister.

CARD

Follow instructions for canister to roll, cut and paint one cat.

Cut a 6½ x 4½-inch rectangle of purple decorative paper; tear along edges, tearing paper toward you with purple side up. Center and adhere purple paper to front of card using paper glue.

Trim a 3 x 4-inch piece of silver handmade paper with decorative-edge scissors. Adhere silver paper to front of card at an angle using instant-dry paper glue. Let dry.

Trim edges of two 1½ x 2-inch rectangles of vellum using decorative-edge scissors. Brush violet paint onto "meow" stamp and stamp image onto one piece of vellum; reapply paint to stamp and stamp other vellum rectangle; let dry. ***Note:** Immediately wash stamp in warm water to remove paint.* Adhere vellum rectangles at an angle in upper right and lower left corners, applying paper glue in the corners only. Let dry.

Using instant-dry paper glue, adhere cat, buttons and confetti hearts to card.

MAGNET

Follow instructions for canister to roll, cut and paint one cat. Trace around finished cat on paper backing of adhesive-backed magnet sheet; cut out, cutting magnet cat slightly smaller than clay cat. Peel off paper backing and press clay cat onto magnetic shape. ■

SOURCES: Air-dry modeling compound from Creative Paperclay; pearlescent paint from Jacquard; adhesives from Beacon.

Precious Pets Magnet Set

Designs by MARY AYRES

Honor your pets by creating these quick-to-make magnets featuring your favorite photos of them.

MATERIALS

- 2 (3½-inch) white slide mounts
- White card stock
- Patterned papers: dark blue mesh and sand
- Clear vellum
- 6 (⅛-inch) round silver eyelets and eyelet-setting tool
- 4 silver mini brads
- 2 silver book plates
- Word rub-on transfers
- 20-gauge tinned copper wire
- White cotton string
- 2 (3-inch-square) pet photos
- Brown dye ink pad
- Corner edger
- Craft sponge
- 1⁄16- and ⅛-inch circle punches
- Magnetic tape
- Instant-dry paper glue
- Computer font (optional)

CAT MAGNET

Trace around slide mount onto blue mesh patterned paper; cut out and adhere to front of slide mount. Round off corners using corner edger. Antique inner and outer edges of slide mount using a small piece of dry sponge and brown ink pad.

Use computer or hand print pet's name on white card stock; cut rectangle around name to fit in bookplate; adhere name to back of bookplate. Position bookplate on bottom of frame; mark positions of holes. Punch 1⁄16-inch holes; attach bookplate using mini brads.

Punch ⅛-inch holes in top corners of frame; set eyelets in holes. Cut a 6-inch piece of wire; thread wire ends through eyelets and twist to hold hanger in place. Adhere strips of magnetic tape to back of frame.

Transfer desired sentiment onto vellum; tear rectangle around word, leaving room to attach an eyelet. Punch a ⅛-inch hole in end of vellum strip; mount eyelet in hole. Thread string through eyelet and tie vellum sentiment to wire hanger.

DOG MAGNET

Follow instructions for cat magnet substituting sand patterned paper for blue mesh. ■

SOURCES: Slide mounts from Design Originals; patterned papers from The Paper Loft and Karen Foster Design; glue from Beacon.

Cool Cat Pin & Card

Design by MEREDITH BRYNTESON, COURTESY OF CLEARSNAP

Is it a card or a gift? It's both! The detachable cat pin becomes a keepsake gift.

Ink recessed areas of cat tile, applying color from red ink pad with inking brush. Wipe off excess with paper towels. Lightly tap antique gold ink pad over tile to ink raised areas. Heat-set to dry ink. Ink edges of tile with red ink pad; heat-set. Let cool.

Fold a 4 x 8-inch rectangle of red card stock to make a 4-inch-square card. Center and adhere a 3-inch square of black card stock to front of card using glue stick. Adhere a 2¼-inch square of gold card stock to front of card at an angle.

Adhere pin back to back of cat tile using double-sided adhesive tape. Punch two holes ½ inch apart in center of a ¾ x 1⅝-inch strip of gold card stock; pin cat tile through holes. Center tile on front of card; adhere one end of the gold card stock strip to card using double-sided adhesive tape.

Stamp sentiment on white card stock using alphabet stamps and red ink pad; cut out. Adhere words to 3-inch square of gold card stock with glue stick. Center and adhere gold card stock on 3½-inch square of black card stock; center and adhere inside card. ■

SOURCES: Cats Style Stones Set, inking brush and ColorBox MicaMagic pigment ink pads from Clearsnap.

MATERIALS

- Sparkle card stock: black, gold and red
- White card stock
- 1¼-inch cultured stone tile engraved with cat design
- Fast-drying pigment ink pads: antique gold and red
- Inking brush
- ⅝-inch alphabet stamps
- 1-inch pin back
- Paper towels
- Heat tool
- ¼-inch circle punch
- Double-sided adhesive tape
- Glue stick

Mother's Day Gift Set

Designs by LORETTA MATEIK

Fun and whimsy abound in this cute gift set just for Mom.

Pouch

Using patterns provided, cut pouch and hat brim from pink card stock; cut face from ivory card stock. Run hat brim and top 1¼ inches of hat (on front only) through crimper.

Score pouch along dashed lines; fold pouch and assemble, applying double-sided tape to side tab and folding up bottom sections. Using the yellow ink pad, stamp small flowers on white card stock; outline flowers and scribble centers using black marker. Using green ink pad, stamp three small leaves on white card stock. Cut out flowers and leaves.

Adhere face to pouch using double-sided tape; add facial details with a black marker. Blush cheeks with chalk. Adhere flower, leaf and feather to hat so that they will peek out from top where brim will be attached. Adhere brim using double-sided tape; adhere remaining flowers and leaves.

Punch two holes in sides of pouch. Thread cord ends through holes; knot inside pouch to hold handle in place. Fill pouch with tissue and a small gift.

MATERIALS

- Card stock: pink, white and ivory/beige
- White tissue gift wrap
- Rubber stamps: small leaf and small flower
- Ink pads: yellow, green and watermark
- Black marker
- Rose chalk
- White cording
- Pink feather
- Paper crimper
- 1⁄16-inch circle punch
- Stylus
- Double-sided tape

Truffle Box

Using patterns provided, cut truffle box and hat brim from beige card stock. Run hat brim and top 1¼ inches of round sections of box through crimper. Score box along dashed lines; punch holes using 1⁄16-inch circle punch. Referring to truffle box assembly diagram, cut face from light ivory card stock.

Using the lavender ink pad, stamp two flowers on white card stock; using the pink ink pad, stamp one flower; using the green ink pad, stamp two small leaves. Cut out flowers and leaves. Use computer or hand print "Happy Mother's Day" on white card stock; trim to ½ x 1 inch.

Fold truffle box and assemble, applying double-sided tape to tabs. Adhere face to box using double-sided tape; add facial details with a black marker. Blush cheeks with chalk. Adhere two flowers and one leaf under top of brim area. Adhere hat brim using double-sided tape; adhere last leaf to brim using double-sided tape. Adhere last flower using adhesive foam dot. Adhere message under face.

Fill box with truffles or a small gift; thread ribbon through holes and tie box closed.

MATERIALS

- Card stock: light ivory, white and beige
- Rubber stamps: small leaf and small flower
- Ink pads: lavender, pink and green
- Black marker
- Rose chalk
- 1⁄16-inch-wide lavender ribbon
- Paper crimper
- 1⁄16-inch circle punch
- Stylus
- Double-sided tape
- Adhesive foam dots
- Computer font (optional)

Wrapping Paper & Tag

WRAPPING PAPER

Very lightly mark gift wrap tissue at 2½-inch intervals horizontally and vertically, but do not draw pencil lines between these points. Using yellow marker, draw lines freehand.

Using the pink ink pad, stamp the solid portion of the two-part flower stamp in every other space; stamp the outline image with black. Stamp a small green leaf by each flower.

Use one, two or more sheets of plain white tissue under the stamped sheet when wrapping gifts. Wrap package with yellow picot-edge ribbon; attach tag.

TAG

Using patterns provided, cut one tag and one hat brim from yellow card stock. Run hat brim and top 2 inches of tag through crimper. Cut face from light ivory card stock.

Using the pink ink pad, stamp the solid portion of the two-part flower stamp on white card stock; stamp the second part of the stamp in black. Cut out. Ink a small area of white card stock with green ink pad; cut two leaf shapes.

Use computer or hand print "Happy Mother's Day" on pink card stock; trim card stock around lettering, tapering it in toward bottom. Adhere face to tag using adhesive dots; add facial details with a black marker. Blush cheeks with chalk. Chalk edges of tag (but not rounded hat portion) and edges of hat brim.

Use small flower stamp and clear ink pad to randomly stamp images on pouch below the face. Add a message to the tag. Adhere hat brim to head using adhesive dots. Using black marker, outline brim and top of hat with a dashed line. Using adhesive dots, adhere leaves and flowers to hat; adhere button in center of flower. Punch hole in top of tag; attach ribbon tie. ■

SOURCES: Rubber stamps, ink pads and chalk from Stampin' Up!; watermark ink pad from Tsukineko.

MATERIALS

- Card stock: yellow, white, light ivory and pink
- White tissue gift wrap
- Rubber stamps: small leaf, two-part large flower and small flower
- Ink pads: pink, green, black and watermark
- Markers: black and yellow
- Rose chalk
- ½-inch black flat button
- 3/16-inch-wide yellow picot-edge ribbon
- Paper crimper
- ⅛-inch circle punch
- Adhesive dots
- Computer font (optional)

DRAWINGS on page 163

Rose Necklace & Card

Design by BETH CLARK, COURTESY OF DUNCAN

Surprise your mom this Mother's Day with a pretty card that holds a delicate rose pendant necklace.

NECKLACE

Adhere the rose rub-on transfer onto the rose quartz pendant. Coat with gloss sealer; let dry.

Attach one half of clasp to beading thread. String beads in order: 71 pearl seed beads, one silver round bead, 27 pink pony beads, three silver round beads and silver seed bead (center). String pendant onto wire so that it rests on seed bead; string remaining beads in reverse order and attach other end of clasp.

CARD

Cut white card stock to measure 4¾ x 14¼ inches. Fold strip in thirds, folding ends toward center, forming three 4¾-inch-square sections. Open the card; flip it over to the other side (back) and press flat.

Beginning on the left, cover the first two sections with rose patterned paper. Cut a 3¼-inch-square opening in center of second (center) section. Flip card over. Cut a 2¾-inch square of rose patterned vellum; center and adhere vellum square on first (left) section. Center and cut two small x's in vellum ¼ inch from top edge and 1¼ inches apart. Thread ends of necklace through x's so pendant hangs in center.

For envelope, cut a 3½-inch square of rose patterned vellum; turn it on the diagonal, wrong side up. Form envelope by folding left and right points till they just meet in center; fold up bottom point to overlap sides; adhere with glue. Fold top point down; crease. Cut small slit in bottom so top point can be inserted to close envelope. Cut two small holes in back of envelope to match holes in card. Feed ends of necklace through holes in back of envelope; adhere envelope to back of card.

Flip card to inside again. Cover center section with pink vellum; cut 3-inch-square window in center.

Stamp "Happy Mother's Day" on third section using pink ink pad. Adhere first and second sections together so finished card has two panels. ■

SOURCES: Tulip rub-on transfers, Aleene's Instant Decoupage Glue, PSX papers, vellum and rubber stamp from Duncan.

MATERIALS

NECKLACE

- 1-inch rose quartz heart pendant
- 1-inch rose rub-on transfer
- 8 (4mm) silver round beads
- Silver seed bead
- 54 pink matte-finish small pony beads
- 142 cream pearl seed beads
- Gloss sealer
- Beading thread
- Brush
- Clasp
- Beading needle

CARD

- White card stock
- Rose patterned paper
- Rose patterned vellum
- Solid pink vellum
- "Happy Mother's Day" rubber stamp
- Pink ink pad
- Craft knife
- Glue stick

Mom's Love Notes

Design by HEATHER D. WHITE

Mothers are sentimental and keep all the cards and notes given to them by their children. Here's a place to store all of her remembrances!

Remove all hinges, clasps and screws from box. Measure and cut lavender patterned paper to cover top and edges of lid. Measure and cut yellow patterned paper to cover sides and bottom of box. Paint box interior, hinges, clasps and screw heads—not threads—with white paint. While paint dries, sand edges and surfaces of all paper pieces cut to fit the box. Adhere paper pieces to box with double-sided tape.

Cut a 4¼ x 3½-inch piece of lavender patterned paper for panel on front of box; cut two daisies from yellow patterned paper and daisy centers from lavender. Sand surfaces and edges of panel, daisies and centers. Adhere daisies and centers to panel with double-sided tape.

Use computer or hand print "Mom's Love Notes" on blank white labels. Cut out words; tint edges with light purple chalk. Adhere words to panel. Punch holes for snaps; set snaps in panel with eyelet-setting tool. Adhere panel to box with double-sided tape. Reassemble box with painted hinges, clasps and screws.

Use computer or hand print headings for tops of card dividers on assorted patterned papers. Cut card dividers to measure 5 x 7 inches. Using manila file folder as a pattern, trim tabs around headings. Sand edges and surfaces of card dividers. Mount card dividers on white card stock with double-sided tape; trim. Insert card dividers in box. ■

SOURCES: Patterned papers from All My Memories; snaps from Making Memories.

MATERIALS

- 5½ x 8 x 6¼-inch wooden box with hinged lid
- Patterned paper: assorted lavenders and yellows
- White card stock
- Blank paper labels or stickers
- 4 silver snaps and eyelet-setting tool
- Light purple chalk
- White acrylic paint
- Manila file folder
- Small Phillips-head screwdriver
- Paintbrush
- Sandpaper
- ⅛-inch circle punch
- Double-sided tape
- Computer font (optional)

Graduation Card

Design by JACKI JONES

Tuck a gift certificate or cash inside this graduation-cap card for a much-appreciated gift.

Form a 5 x 7-inch card with fold at top from light-color card stock. Using patterns provided, trim card in the shape of a mortarboard. Lay card facedown on wrong side of darker textured card stock; trace around card onto card stock. Cut out, cutting slightly outside traced lines. Adhere card stock to front of card using adhesive foam dots.

Cut mortarboard top from medium-color textured card stock. Punch hole in center; loop tassel around brad and set brad in hole. Adhere mortarboard top to card using adhesive foam dots.

Stamp "Congratulations" and diploma on vellum using pigment ink; sprinkle with clear embossing powder and emboss. Tear out "Congratulations"; cut out diploma. Adhere "Congratulations" across bottom of card using vellum tape.

Stamp numbers of graduation year at bottom of card stock tag using pigment ink. Adhere vellum diploma to tag using vellum tape. Thread tassel through string loop on tag; adhere tag to mortarboard using adhesive foam dots. ■

SOURCES: Rubber stamps and anywhere punch from Stampin' Up!.

DRAWINGS on page 166

MATERIALS

- Textured card stock in medium and dark shades of desired color
- Card stock in a lighter complementary color for inside of card
- Clear vellum
- White card stock tag
- Brad
- Tassel
- Rubber stamps
- Pigment ink
- Clear embossing powder
- ⅛-inch anywhere hole punch
- Vellum tape
- Adhesive foam dots

Graduation Pocket Card

Design by LISA ROJAS

Gift cards or cash can be tucked in among the cellophane shreds for a surprise gift to the new graduate!

MATERIALS

Card stock: dark blue, white and silver
Patterned papers: star print and blue stripe
Colored pencils
Rubber stamps: teddy bear, 2- and 1-inch mortarboards, 2½-inch diploma, 1½ x 3⅜-inch "Congrats!"
Black dye ink pad
Metallic gold marker
15/16-inch-wide dark blue ribbon with metallic gold thread
Finely shredded raffia: white and silver
Decorative-edge scissors
Circle punch
Spray sealer
½-inch adhesive foam squares
Craft glue
Permanent adhesive applicator and cartridges

Stamp teddy bear, smaller mortarboard and diploma twice each on white card stock using black ink pad. Color teddy bears and mortarboards identically using colored pencils; color ribbons on diplomas using metallic gold marker. Spray images with sealer; when dry, cut out. Glue mortarboard and small diploma to bears' outstretched hands. Adhere one bear over the other using adhesive foam squares to give the image a 3-D effect.

CONTINUED on page 85

Father's Day Magnets

Designs by JEANNE WYNHOFF

Fishing themed paper and jute cord go hand in hand to create these unique magnets that Dad will love.

MATERIALS

- Brown or tan laminate chips:
  - 1 (3½ x 5 inches) and
  - 2 (1¾ x 2 inches)
- Patterned papers
- White card stock
- Fishing-theme card stock stickers
- Wood-look alphabet tiles
- Fishing creel sticker
- Cork sheet
- Fine jute twine
- Tan decorative fiber
- Tree buttons
- Round mini brads
- Black ink pad
- Stamping sponge
- 1-inch "D" stencil
- Craft knife
- Label maker with ⅜-inch-wide adhesive black label tape
- Magnetic tape
- Adhesive
- Adhesive dots
- Dimensional adhesive dots

LARGE MAGNET

Apply adhesive to the Formica surface of the 3½ x 5-inch laminate chip. Adhere a torn piece of patterned paper over one area of tag; adhere additional papers, overlapping edges, until chip is covered. Trim edges with scissors. Ink edges of chip with black ink using stamping sponge.

Stencil "D" near top of tag in center using stamping sponge and black ink pad; complete "Dad" by adding A and D alphabet tiles.

CONTINUED on page 85

Fish Trinket Box

Design by KATHLEEN PANEITZ

Forgo the traditional tie or money clip and give dad a unique gift this year. This mini trinket box will hold a variety of treasures, including a gift card to his favorite sporting goods store.

MATERIALS

Oval papier-mâché box with lid
Fish patterned paper
Thin cork sheet or cork patterned paper
Natural hemp cord
Brown fly-fishing fly with spinner
3⅓-inch resin fish
Decoupage medium
Paper trimmer (optional)
Straight pins or small spring clothespins (optional)
Adhesive dots

Trace around top of box lid onto fish patterned paper. Cut out oval; adhere to top of lid with decoupage medium. Cut a strip of fish patterned paper to cover sides of box; adhere to box with decoupage medium.

Cut a strip of cork to cover sides of lid; adhere to lid with decoupage medium. If desired, use straight pins or spring clothespins to hold cork in place until decoupage medium dries.

Wrap a double strand of hemp cord around sides of lid; thread fly onto one strand of cord, then knot strands tightly on front. ***Note:** This can be done immediately after adhering the cork to the lid to help hold it in place.* Adhere resin fish in center of lid using adhesive dots. ■

SOURCES: Patterned paper from K&Company; cork paper from Magenta; resin fish from Heartland Crafts.

Bridal Guest Book

Design by SUSAN HUBER

Keep track of all the wedding guests with a simple composition notebook embellished with romantic accents such as flowers and lace.

MATERIALS

- Composition book
- Patterned papers:
  - complementary florals and lace
- "Love" patterned transparency
- Square letter brads
- Metal word plates
- Mini brads
- 2-inch-wide twill tape
- White fringed fiber
- Lace scraps
- Silk flowers
- Keys-with-heart charm
- Pink chalk
- Craft knife
- Paper piercer
- Sewing needle and thread
- Craft cement
- Double-sided tacky tape

***Project note:** Adhere elements using double-sided tacky tape unless instructed otherwise.*

Cover book spine with twill tape. Measure and cut floral patterned paper to fit on front cover of book; adhere. Repeat on back cover.

Cut a 3-inch-wide strip of another floral patterned paper as long as book cover; tear along right edge. Chalk torn edge; adhere strip to left side of front cover, next to spine. Measure and cut transparency to fit on front cover; adhere over patterned papers using tiny dots of craft cement. Punch holes through cover using paper piercer; attach metal word plates using mini brads.

Cut lace to cover twill spine and left third of front cover. Gather lace in center of right edge using needle and thread. Adhere lace to front cover and over spine along top and bottom edges. Set mini brads through centers of silk flowers to attach flowers to cover at gathered area of lace. Adhere lace at corners of front cover. Adhere silk flowers over lace using mini brads.

Wrap fibers around flower clusters; "hang" keys-and-heart charm from fibers in upper right corner; adhere charm on cover using craft cement. Punch holes through cover in upper left corner using paper piercer; attach square letter brads to spell "GUESTS."

Cover inside of back and front covers with patterned papers. ■

SOURCES: Patterned paper from K&Company; transparency from Creative Imaginations; letter brads and metal word plates from Colorbök; gold leafing pen from Krylon.

FRIENDS ~
SHARING WITH US
BLESSED DAY.
Lisa Taormina
APRIL 16, 2004

Wedding Favor Tag Book

Design by JULIE RYVER

Let all your wedding guests know you cherish them with a handmade favor book. Containing a picture of the happy couple, this is a great way for guests to remember your special day.

Using template or die cutter, create two 3 x 5-inch tags from embossed black card stock and one each from embossed ivory vellum, embossed ivory card stock and filigree print paper. Stack tags face up, with embossed black card stock tag on the bottom for back cover, then filigree print paper, embossed ivory card stock and embossed ivory vellum tags. Top with remaining embossed black card stock tag.

Cut a 9- and a 6-inch piece each from sheer black and sheer silver ribbon. Hold 9-inch pieces together and fold them in half; push center loop through holes in tags from back to front. Hold 6-inch pieces together and thread them through loop on front of book, centering them. On back of book, pull 9-inch ribbons snug; knot. Trim ribbon ends at an angle.

Cut two 2⅛-inch squares plain black card stock; use them to mat photo on embossed ivory card stock tag; adhere with glue stick. Adhere floral photo corner in lower right corner of photo. Use computer or hand print message on plain ivory card stock; decorate corners with corner punch. Use glue stick to adhere message to filigree print tag.

Use wire cutters to remove shank from heart button; use adhesive dot to adhere button in bottom right corner of cover. ■

SOURCES: Embossed card stock and vellum from K&Company; filigree print paper from Making Memories; photo corner from EK Success.

MATERIALS

- Embossed card stock: black and ivory
- Plain card stock: black and ivory
- Embossed ivory vellum
- Gray-on-black filigree print paper
- Floral photo corner
- 2⅛-inch-square photo
- Silver heart shank button
- ⅝-inch-wide sheer ribbon: silver and black
- 3 x 5-inch tag template or die cutter
- Decorative corner punch
- Wire cutters
- Glue stick
- Adhesive dot
- Computer font (optional)

Anniversary Tin

Design by SUSAN HUBER

Take a journey down memory lane by honoring a wedding anniversary with an altered tin.

Adhere patterned paper to lid of tin. Adhere lace over lower corners. Adhere alphabet stickers to round tags to spell "our memories"; top some letters with acrylic "pebble" stickers; affix tags to lid. Adhere epoxy word stickers. Stick mini brads through centers of silk flowers; fold ends flat on back; adhere flowers to lid. Wrap fibers around flowers; adhere key-and-heart charm to lid.

Paint back of tin with gesso; let dry. Streak with metallic paints; let dry.

Cut card stock to form accordion-style pages. Each page should measure 4¾ x 5½ inches; piece card stock together as desired. ***Note:*** *Sample project has six and one-quarter pages; the quarter-page folds over onto the last page as a flap, providing a place to add personalization.* Adhere first page inside tin cover; adhere last page inside tin back.

Decorate pages as desired using the following: photos, cut or torn pieces from patterned papers, ephemera such as wedding invitations and poems, charms, snippets of lace and ribbon, and assorted stickers. Mat photos on contrasting card stock or paper as desired; add silver photo corners. Outline each page with silver leafing pen. ■

SOURCES: Patterned papers from K&Company, silver leafing pen from Krylon; metallic paints from Jacquard.

MATERIALS

- CD tin
- Patterned papers: floral and word prints
- Assorted card stocks
- Poems, wedding invitation and other ephemera
- 11/16-inch self-adhesive round metal-rim tags
- 2-inch metal-rim heart tag
- 9/16-inch round alphabet stickers
- Acrylic word stickers
- Acrylic "pebble" stickers
- Lace scraps and small lace motifs
- Silk flowers
- Silver leafing pen
- White fringed fiber
- Key-with-heart charm
- Silver photo corners
- Yellow mini brads
- Gesso
- Metallic paints
- Paintbrush
- Craft knife
- Sewing needle and thread
- Clear-drying craft glue
- Foam tape

Key to my heart

Bridal Bliss

Designs by LISA ROJAS

Add an extra touch of romance to a wedding celebration with this pretty floral set, complete with decorations and invitations.

Invitation

Use a computer to print text on lace patterned vellum. Use olive green ink pad and fancy corner rubber stamp to stamp an image in each corner of vellum.

Cut a 6¼ x 5¼-inch rectangle of green card stock and a 6 x 5-inch rectangle of cream card stock. Using applicator and permanent adhesive cartridge, center and adhere cream card stock to green card stock.

Center printed vellum on cream card stock. Using eyelet-setting tool and two eyelets, adhere vellum to card stock, centering eyelets near top edge. Thread green ribbon through eyelets; tie ends on printed side of invitation.

Cut 6 x 10½-inch rectangles of rose patterned paper and cream paper. Using applicator and permanent adhesive cartridge, adhere rose patterned paper to cream paper. Lay rose/cream papers rose side down; fold in sides to meet in center. Using eyelet-setting tool, center and set an eyelet on each side where edges meet.

Insert invitation in rose/cream folder. Thread sheer ivory ribbon through eyelets in rose/cream folder; tie in a bow. Slide stem of silk rose under bow. ■

SOURCES: Patterned paper from Frances Meyer Inc.; rubber stamp by Penny Black; permanent adhesive cartridges and applicator from Xyron.

MATERIALS

- Card stock: green and cream
- Lace patterned white vellum
- Rose patterned paper
- Cream paper
- Ribbon: sheer ivory and complementary green
- Silk rose on a stem
- 4 gold eyelets and eyelet-setting tool
- Fancy corner rubber stamp
- Olive green ink pad
- Permanent adhesive applicator and cartridges
- Computer font

Candle Lamp

Using applicator and permanent adhesive cartridge, coat back of rose patterned paper with permanent adhesive; adhere to card stock. Trace lamp-shade pattern onto card-stock side. Cut out lamp shade and assemble.

Using hot-glue gun, adhere rose trim around top and bottom edges of shade; tie a bow of sheer ribbon and adhere to top edge.

Tie complementary solid and sheer ribbons in a bow around stem of champagne flute. Using needle and thread, tack charm onto bow. Using hot-glue gun, adhere silk rose to bow.

Fill champagne flute ¾ full with water. Float candle on surface. Top champagne flute with lamp shade. ■

SOURCES: Patterned paper from Frances Meyer Inc.; lamp shade pattern from Stampassions; permanent adhesive cartridges and applicator from Xyron.

MATERIALS

- Tan card stock
- Rose patterned paper
- Lamp-shade pattern
- Champagne flute
- Rose trim
- Ribbon: sheer ivory and complementary solid color
- Silk rose
- Gold charm
- Tea-light candle
- Sewing needle and ivory all-purpose thread
- Permanent adhesive applicator and cartridges
- Hot-glue gun with glue sticks

Party Favor

Using applicator and permanent adhesive cartridge, adhere rose patterned paper to white card stock. Trace pattern for pillow box onto card stock side; cut out and assemble pillow box.

Scuff shrink plastic with sandpaper. Using olive green ink, stamp frame onto shrink plastic. Cut out; punch a 1⁄16-inch hole in the top. Using black fine-tip permanent marker, write bride and groom's names inside frame. Shrink frame with heat tool. Mount jump ring in hole.

Fill pillow box with candy or other favors; fold ends closed. Wrap sheer ivory ribbon around pillow box in both directions; tie ends in a bow. Using needle and thread, tack jump ring of charm to ribbon. Slide stem of silk rose under bow. ■

SOURCES: Patterned paper from Frances Meyer Inc.; frame rubber stamp by All Night Media/Plaid; permanent adhesive cartridges and applicator from Xyron.

MATERIALS

- White card stock
- Rose patterned paper
- Pillow box pattern
- Frosted shrink plastic
- Sheer ivory ribbon
- Silk rose on a stem
- Gold jump ring
- Frame rubber stamp
- Olive green ink pad
- Black fine-tip permanent marker
- Sandpaper
- Heat tool
- 1⁄16-inch circle hole punch
- Sewing needle and ivory all-purpose thread
- Permanent adhesive applicator and cartridges

Father's Day Magnets

CONTINUED FROM PAGE 75

Adhere larger card stock stickers to white card stock; cut out. Leave smaller card stock stickers as they are. Set mini brad in small rectangle of cork; adhere cork in upper left corner using adhesive dot; set mini brads in upper corners of a larger card stock motif; adhere in lower left corner. Separate a single ply from jute twine; cut 3½-inch piece. Wind jute around brads.

Loop decorative fiber through hole in tag-shaped card stock sticker; adhere tag off right edge of magnet. Adhere buttons and smaller motifs to magnet as desired using adhesive dots for some elements and dimensional adhesive dots for others. Adhere magnetic tape on back.

SMALL MAGNETS

Apply adhesive and adhere patterned papers to smaller laminate chips as directed for large magnet; ink edges with black ink. Arrange stickers, buttons, cork embellishments and other components as desired. Spell out words with alphabet tiles, or print out on black tape using label maker. Add mini brads, decorative fiber and jute twine as accents. Add depth by adhering selected elements with dimensional adhesive dots. Adhere magnetic tape to the back of each magnet. ■

SOURCES: Patterned papers from Sweetwater, Karen Foster Design and Daisy D's Paper Co.; stickers from Karen Foster Design and EK Success; cork from LazerLetterz.

Graduation Pocket Card

CONTINUED FROM PAGE 74

From dark blue card stock form a 4¼ x 5½-inch card with fold at the top. Using applicator and permanent adhesive cartridge, center and adhere a 1½ x 5½-inch strip of blue striped paper across front of card ¼ inch below fold; center and adhere a 4 x 5¼-inch rectangle of blue striped paper inside card where one would normally write a message; center and adhere a 4 x 5¼-inch rectangle of blue star patterned paper inside card's front flap.

With card closed and fold at top, fold up lower left and right corners of card's front flap until they meet in center, exposing triangles of blue star patterned paper. Crease folds. Punch a hole in each corner; thread ribbon through holes and tie in a bow, creating pocket.

Adhere teddy bear at center top of card using scrapbooking glue. Mat name card on dark blue card stock; trim edges with decorative-edge scissors; glue larger mortarboard to upper right corner. Adhere name card at an angle to right of bear.

Stamp "Congrats!" on white card stock using black ink pad; cut out, trimming close to letters. Mat lettering on silver card stock, then dark blue card stock. Adhere at upper left corner of card using scrapbooking glue. Adhere one large diploma overlapping left side of teddy bear; adhere remaining diploma in lower right corner of card. Fill card pocket with silver and white raffia shreds. ■

SOURCES: Striped paper from Provo Craft; permanent adhesive cartridges and applicator from Xyron.

July Through September

Give a gift just for the joy of seeing someone smile when they receive it. Whether you choose to greet your child's new teacher or simply let someone know you care, one of these terrific projects fits the bill!

True
friends
True friend
remain true
always
forever

happy
day

A
B
C

Seashells Portfolio

Designs by SUSAN HUBER

Seashells by the seashore grace the front of a small portfolio full of coordinating note cards. Don't like seashells? Substitute your favorite stamp image!

MATERIALS

- Card stock: sky blue, navy blue and brown
- 4 manila note card envelopes
- Seashells rubber stamps
- Ink pads: champagne metallic, watermark and tea-dye
- Gold leafing pen
- Tan craft foam
- Starfish charm
- ⅞-inch-wide bronze metallic organza ribbon
- Blue ⅛-inch eyelets and eyelet-setting tool
- ⅛-inch circle punch
- Die cutter with sand-dollar die
- Ruler and pencil
- Embossing heat tool
- Glue stick
- Foam tape
- Adhesive dots

PORTFOLIO

Trim sky blue card stock to measure 11 x 8½ inches. Fold in half, and then into quarters; crease. Unfold. Position card stock with short edges at top and bottom. On each side edge, mark a point 1 inch below the horizontal fold. Draw lines from those points to the center of the bottom edge (where vertical fold begins). Trim off card stock along those diagonal lines.

Using watermark ink pad, stamp seashells randomly over both sides of card stock; repeat using champagne ink pad. Using gold leafing pen, edge card stock and trace vertical center fold.

Fold point up. Punch a hole ¼ inch from each side edge 1¾ inches above horizontal fold; set eyelets in holes. Fold card stock along center with point on outside, forming a book with two outer diagonal pockets. Turn book so that vertical fold is on the right-hand side.

Cut a 2½-inch square of navy blue card stock; edge with gold leafing pen. Cut a 2-inch square of sky blue card stock; rub edges and surface over tea-dye ink pad. Center and adhere sky blue square on navy blue square using glue stick. Cut a 2-inch square of craft foam; heat with embossing heat tool until foam is soft; stamp seashell in soft foam; let cool. Trim foam to 1⅝ inches square; center and adhere on sky blue card stock using glue stick. Adhere card stock/foam panel to center front of folder, over diagonal edge, using glue stick. Adhere starfish charm in corner of craft foam square using an adhesive dot.

NOTE CARDS

For each of four note cards, fold a 7 x 5-inch piece of navy blue card stock in half to make a 3½ x 5-inch note card. Edge with gold leafing pen. Cut sky blue card stock 3 x 4¼ inches; rub over tea-dye ink pad. Center and adhere sky blue card stock on front of note card using glue stick.

Edge a 1½-inch square of navy card stock with gold leafing pen; adhere to front of note card using foam tape. Punch a sand dollar from brown card stock; edge lightly using gold leafing pen; center and adhere sand dollar to navy blue square using glue stick.

Tuck two cards and two envelopes in each folio pocket. Thread ribbon through eyelets; wrap around portfolio and tie in a bow. ■

SOURCES: Die cutter and die from QuicKutz; stamp from JudiKins; watermark ink pad from Tsukineko Inc.; leafing pen from Krylon.

Dance Like a Flamingo

Design by SUSAN STRINGFELLOW

Celebrate an uninhibited friend who lives life to the fullest by presenting her with a fun reminder of why you love her!

Project note: *Adhere elements using paper glaze unless instructed otherwise.*

Sand both sides of CD so that adhesive will adhere. Cut green patterned card stock to cover front of CD; adhere to CD using liquid adhesive. Lightly sand edges.

Sand edges of a 2 x 5-inch piece of striped patterned paper; adhere across bottom of CD, ¾ inch from edge. Adhere a 2-inch square of pink dotted mesh to left side of CD. Rub edges of a 1½-inch square of cocktails patterned paper over black ink pad; adhere in center of pink dotted mesh. Rub edges of flamingo image over black ink pad; adhere to right side of CD.

Using alphabet stamps and black ink, stamp "dance like a FLAMINGO" across top of CD. Using foam stamps and black acrylic paint, stamp decorative images off edges of CD on right and left. Adhere metal "FUN" tile at center bottom of cocktail paper square and pink dotted mesh.

Wrap two 5-inch lengths of decorative fiber across CD; adhere ends on back. Bend both tabs on flower brads in the same direction to attach them across bottom edge of CD; add dots of paper glaze to secure brads. Adhere magnets on back of CD. ■

SOURCES: Card stock, foam stamps and brads from Making Memories; patterned paper from Doodlebug Design Inc. and Treehouse Designs; image from Altered Pages; self-adhesive mesh from Magic Mesh; stamps from Hero Arts and Rubber Stamp Ave.; metal tile from Kay; paper glaze from JudiKins.

MATERIALS

- CD
- Green patterned card stock
- Patterned papers: stripes and cocktails
- Paper flamingo image
- Pink "dotted" self-adhesive mesh
- Decorative foam stamps
- ¼-inch alphabet stamps
- Black ink pad
- Black acrylic paint
- Bright flower brads
- Metal "FUN" tile
- Decorative fibers
- Fine sandpaper
- Craft knife
- Magnets
- Paper glaze
- Paper adhesive

Mini Travel Notebook

Design by JULIE JANSEN

Just before you say "Bon voyage," present that special someone with a notebook in which to record all his travel adventures.

Cut patterned paper to cover front and back covers of composition book; apply adhesive to back of paper and adhere to composition book. Trim off excess paper.

Apply adhesive to back of jute ribbon; cover spine of composition book with jute ribbon; trim off excess. Using gold leafing pen, add a thin gold edge around edges of covers.

Adhere travel stickers and word stickers to cover. Wrap organdy ribbon around front cover near spine; tie ends in a bow on center front. ■

SOURCES: Decorative paper from 7gypsies; stickers from EK Success and All My Memories; ribbon from Aldik; leafing pen from Krylon; adhesive cartridge and applicator from Xyron.

MATERIALS

- Mini composition book
- Travel-print decorative paper
- Travel-theme stickers
- Travel word stickers
- 5 inches burgundy jute ribbon
- 15-inch sheer white organdy ribbon with gold stars
- Gold leafing pen
- Adhesive cartridge with applicator

Vacation
MEMORIES

Vacation Memories Frame

Design by JEANNE WYNHOFF

Choose a favorite vacation photo and embellish it with coordinating papers and memorabilia from that special trip!

MATERIALS

- Patterned papers: tan, blue and seashore prints
- Tan card stock
- 10 x 8-inch wooden frame
- Acrylic craft paint: dark blue and off-white
- Crackle medium
- Seashore sticker sheet
- "Vacation" sticker
- Alphabet stickers
- Decorative fibers
- ¾ x 1½-inch rectangular metal-rimmed tag
- Gold and copper seashore charms
- Small seashells
- Fishnet
- 1-inch foam paintbrushes
- Photo
- Adhesive squares
- Adhesive foam dots
- Hot-glue gun and glue sticks

Project note: *Adhere paper and other elements using adhesive squares unless otherwise instructed.*

Remove backing from frame. Paint frame dark blue using foam brush; let dry. Coat with crackle medium; let dry. Paint with off-white paint; let dry.

Cut tan card stock to cover cardboard backing inside frame, trimming as needed so that backing can be reinserted. Adhere card stock to frame backing.

Cut a 5½-inch square of blue patterned paper; adhere to card stock in upper right corner. Cut a piece of tan paper 8 x 10 inches; tear off upper right corner on the diagonal, beginning about 5 inches from corner. Adhere tan paper over background so that blue patterned paper is visible in upper right-hand corner, behind torn corner.

Cut a vertical border strip approximately 10 x 2½ inches from seashore sticker sheet; adhere along left edge of frame backing. Replace backing in frame.

Cut tan paper 3½ x 4¾ inches; tear along right edge. Adhere in upper right corner ½ inch from top and 1 inch from right-hand edge. Cut blue patterned paper 5¾ x 5⅛ inches; tear diagonally across the bottom from right edge down to left corner; adhere over tan paper, leaving ⅛-inch tan border along top and right-hand edges.

Trim photo to 4 x 4¾ inches; adhere to 3½ x 4⅞-inch tan paper, leaving ⅛-inch-wide tan border along top and right-hand edges; adhere matted photo to blue paper in frame, leaving ⅛-inch blue border along top and right-hand edges. Adhere alphabet stickers to spell "Memories" along torn bottom edge of blue paper.

Thread fibers through hole in metal-rimmed tag; adhere "Vacation" sticker to tag. Adhere a seashell sticker at lower left corner of photo; overlay with tag; adhere top portion of tag using an adhesive foam dot. Hot-glue a charm and small shell to bottom of tag. Arrange fiber up side of photo; secure with dots of hot glue.

Adhere seashell stickers on the diagonal down right side of photo. Arrange seashells in lower right corner of frame, overlapping some for dimension. Hot-glue shells in place, gluing some to the frame itself.

Cut a 6-inch square of fishnet; adhere on the diagonal over seashells and bottom right corner of the frame using dots of hot glue, concealing dots of glue under seashells and charms. Add more shells and charms as desired. Trim excess net and knots that would keep the frame from standing evenly. ■

SOURCES: Patterned papers from Hot Off The Press and Carolee's Creations; tag from Making Memories; stickers from Sweetwater, Bo-Bunny Press and Provo Craft.

Thinking of You Tin

Design by MARY AYRES

Add some pretty embellishments to a recycled CD tin and give it to a friend as an unexpected gift.

Spray both halves of CD tin with black spray paint.

Cut a 5¼ x 4⅝-inch piece of black card stock. Cut one 2⅝ x 2⁵⁄₁₆-inch piece from each of four patterned papers; adhere patterned papers to black card stock, butting edges. Trim corners with corner punch.

Using sewing machine threaded with gold thread, zigzag around edges of patterned paper pieces. Rub over stitched edges with brown ink pad for "antiqued" appearance. Adhere stitched panel to lid.

Place gift in tin. Wrap hemp cord diagonally around tin, tying ends in a bow in upper right corner. Adhere skeleton leaves to tin with stem ends under bow.

For tag, use computer font or hand print "Thinking of You" on remaining patterned paper; trim to measure ¾ x 3 inches, positioning words toward left. Rub edges with brown ink pad. Center and adhere on 1⅛ x 3⅜-inch rectangle torn from handmade paper. Using sewing machine threaded with gold thread, straight stitch around printed tag ⅛-inch from edge. Punch ⅛-inch circle in right end of tag; set copper eyelet in hole. Thread gold pearl cotton through eyelet; tie to hemp cord bow. Adhere button stickers to tag; adhere tag to lid.

Lightly sand copper heart charm. Thread gold pearl cotton through hole; tie to hemp cord bow. ■

SOURCES: Patterned papers, charm and stickers from K&Company; spray paint from Krylon; Fabri-Tac adhesive from Beacon.

MATERIALS

- 5½ x 4⅞-inch metal CD tin
- Black card stock
- 5 complementary patterned papers
- Neutral-color handmade paper
- 2 plum skeleton leaves
- Copper "hope" heart tag
- 3 domed button stickers
- ⅛-inch round copper eyelet and eyelet-setting tool
- Gold metallic pearl cotton
- Fine hemp cord
- Flat black spray paint
- Brown ink pad
- Decorative corner punch
- ⅛-inch circle punch
- Sewing machine and gold metallic thread
- Fine sandpaper
- Permanent adhesive
- Computer font (optional)

True Friends CD

Design by JEANNE WYNHOFF

Remind a friend how much you appreciate her with the gift of an altered CD!

MATERIALS

- CD
- White card stock
- Yellow patterned paper
- "Friendship" punch-outs
- Alphabet stickers
- Decorative fibers
- ⅜-inch sheer brown polka-dot ribbon
- Alphabet foam stamps
- Brown chalk ink pad
- Silver brad
- 4 silver jump rings
- Silk flower
- Brown fine-tip marker
- White gel pen
- Fine sandpaper
- Nail file
- Small pliers
- Needle
- ⅛-inch circle punch
- Cotton-tip swab or makeup sponge
- Adhesive dots
- Glue

Thoroughly sand surface of CD with sandpaper so that glue will adhere. Cut a circle of white card stock to cover back of CD; adhere using glue. Cut a circle of yellow patterned paper to cover front of CD; adhere using glue. Using a brown fine-tip marker, add tiny dots around CD close to edge; rub edge of CD on brown chalk ink pad.

Using foam stamps and brown chalk ink pad, stamp "friends" toward top of CD. Draw dots down centers of letters using white gel pen. Add alphabet stickers to spell "True" up left edge.

Use scissors or nail file to remove nibs where tag and flower punch-outs were attached to sheet; rub edges of punch-outs on chalk ink pad. Using a needle, punch two holes 1 inch apart in center bottom edge of tag, and a hole in the top of each flower. Suspend flowers from tags using jump rings.

Using the circle punch, punch a hole in tag; thread fibers through hole and adhere tag to CD using adhesive dots. Tie small bow from ribbon; adhere to left side of tag using an adhesive dot.

Remove the center from the silk flower; separate two layers of petals. Using a cotton-tip swab or makeup sponge, ink top petals with brown chalk ink, beginning in the center and working out. Poke brad through center of silk flower; adhere to CD to right of tag using an adhesive dot. ■

SOURCES: Patterned paper from Provo Craft; chalk ink pad from Clearsnap; stamps from Making Memories.

Encouragement Key Chains

Designs by SANDRA GRAHAM SMITH

Let a friend know how much you care by presenting her with a tiny key chain emblazoned with a kind sentiment.

"JOY"

Stamp white tissue with collage stamp using pearl green ink. Spread laminating liquid on laminate chip; lay stamped tissue over top and press tissue into liquid; tear away excess tissue. Apply more laminating liquid on sides and spread a thin layer on top.

Stamp "Joy" sentiment on top of key chain using black ink pad; let dry. Ink edges and draw border around front of key chain using silver leafing pen.

Using key punch, punch largest key from aluminum sheet; cut off top of key and position over hole in key chain; adhere using craft cement. Snip prongs off dragonfly brad using wire cutters; adhere brad in bottom corner of key chain using craft cement. Thread key chain onto split ring.

"GRATITUDE"

Follow instructions for "Joy" key ring substituting light blue tissue for white and "Gratitude" stamp for "Joy." ■

SOURCES: Stamps from Stamper's Anonymous and Hero Arts; leafing pen from Krylon; laminating medium from Duncan; craft cement from Eclectic Products Inc.; key punch from Punch Bunch.

MATERIALS

- 2 (1¾ x 2⅝-inch) laminate chips
- Tissue paper: light blue and white
- Small sheet of aluminum craft metal
- Rubber stamps: collage, "Joy" and "Gratitude"
- Ink pads: pearl green and black
- Silver leafing pen
- 2 silver dragonfly brads
- Key punch
- Wire cutters
- 2 split rings
- Laminating medium
- Craft cement

Welcome Home

Design by SAHILY GONZALEZ

Decorate a new house or apartment with a personalized door hanger, complete with assorted fibers and embellishments.

Cover all but top and bottom ⅝ inch of door hanger with word-print paper; adhere green metallic paper along top and bottom edges. Trim paper edges even with door hanger using craft knife.

Adhere "There's no Place like Home" sticker over bottom strip of green metallic paper. Adhere "Home Sweet Home" image in lower right-hand corner of word-print paper. Adhere "peace" tile to left of "Home Sweet Home" image and slightly higher.

Turn door hanger so that right edge is at bottom. Spell "HOME" along bottom (right) edge using larger black alphabet stickers; overlay pink square "h" sticker over "H" and "O," and pink square "m" sticker over "M" and "E."

Attach house-shaped wire clip over left edge of door hanger. Use ¼-inch alphabet stamps and black ink to stamp "welcome" on door hanger inside house-shaped wire clip.

Punch a hole in one tip of the cork triangle; tie fibers through hole, then tie triangle around left edge of opening, threading key charm onto the fibers. Adhere cork triangle to door hanger; add more fibers as desired. ■

SOURCES: Patterned paper from Doodlebug Design Inc.; metallic paper from Paper Adventures; paper image from K&Company; pink alphabet stickers and word tile from Creative Imaginations; black alphabet stickers from Sticker Studio; clear sticker from EK Success; PSX stamps from Duncan.

MATERIALS

- Wooden door hanger
- Patterned papers: green metallic, home-theme word print
- "Home Sweet Home" paper image
- Alphabet stickers: ⅝-inch pink squares and 1½-inch black-and-white
- Clear "There's no Place like Home" sticker
- "peace" word tile
- ¼-inch lowercase alphabet rubber stamps
- Black ink pad
- House-shaped wire clip
- Small key charm
- 1-inch cork triangle
- Decorative fibers
- Craft knife
- ⅛-inch circle punch
- Adhesive

Floral Address Book

Design by JEANNE WYNHOFF

MATERIALS

- 6 x 6$\frac{3}{16}$ x 1$\frac{1}{8}$-inch ring-bound address book
- Textured card stock: rose and pale pink
- Decorative fibers
- Floral paper punch-outs
- Quotation and alphabet stickers
- 4$\frac{1}{4}$-inch x 2$\frac{3}{4}$-inch foam rose stamp
- Deep pink ink pad
- Complementary pink chalks
- Floral charm with gold jump ring
- Double-sided tape
- Glue dots
- Adhesive squares

Choose colorful papers to cover a standard address book. This is one that won't be hidden away in a drawer!

Project note: *Adhere elements using double-sided tape unless instructed otherwise.*

Cover front and back covers of address book with separate pieces of rose card stock, folding edges to inside and mitering corners; adhere. Cut pale pink card stock 6½ x 3½ inches; tear off ¼ inch along each long side. Cover spine of address book with strip, folding ends to inside and mitering as needed. Adhere.

Cover insides of covers with rectangles of rose card stock.

CONTINUED on page 167

Recipe Card Magnet

Design by JEANNE WYNHOFF

This unique gift preserves a favorite family recipe and makes a great addition to a gift basket containing all the ingredients to create the recipe!

Cut brown card stock 8½ x 5¼ inches; create a ¼-inch-tall tab in upper left corner by rounding outer corner, cutting straight across for 1½ inches, then rounding other corner and cutting across to right-hand edge. In lower right-hand corner, round the outer corner, cut straight across (toward left) for 3½ inches, then round other corner and cut across to left-hand edge. Fold up bottom of folder so that top of bottom tab is even with top folder edge, not top tab edge.

CONTINUED on page 119

MATERIALS

- 2 (3½ x 5-inch) laminate chips
- Brown textured card stock
- Tan smooth card stock
- Hershey chocolate stickers and punch-outs
- Small photos
- Brown chalk ink pad
- Chalks
- Decorative fibers
- Twill tape
- Paper clips
- Adhesive dots
- Adhesive squares
- Hot-glue gun and glue sticks
- Adhesive-backed magnet strips
- Computer fonts (optional)

OUR
HOME
Crisp Air Crisp

Seasonal Wall Plaque

Designs by SUSAN STRINGFELLOW

Decorating for the seasons is simple with this tiny wall plaque featuring interchangeable floral pieces for each season.

***Project note:** Use matte decoupage medium as glue unless instructed otherwise.*

PLAQUE

Remove and discard cord that comes with plaque. Crumple a 7-inch square of brown fabric patterned paper; smooth out and adhere to front and sides of plaque. Trim paper using a craft knife to expose original eyelets.

Tear a small piece of music patterned paper; adhere in upper center of plaque. Lightly rub the paper's surface with brown dye ink.

Stamp border image along left edge of plaque using brown ink pad. Stamp "HOME" at center top of plaque using 9⁄16-inch rubber stamps and brown ink pad; stamp "OUR" above it and to left using ¼-inch rubber stamps and black ink pad.

Adhere a 3 x 1-inch piece of brown mesh to upper left side of plaque. Adhere green tassel fringe across bottom and over edges of plaque using craft glue; insert an upholstery tack at each end.

Tear some areas and edges on a 2½-inch x 4½-inch piece of corrugated paper. Dry-brush corrugated surface with white paint; sand lightly. Adhere corrugated paper to right side of plaque, above trim.

Use computer or hand print a reversed capital "S" on wheat card stock. Cut out; rub right side lightly with olive and brown dye inks. Adhere to plaque over brown mesh.

Peel backing from a 1½-inch piece of the hook portion of hook-and-loop tape; adhere horizontally to plaque, just above corrugated paper and ¾ inch from right edge.

Braid together three 10-inch lengths of decorative fiber; thread ends through eyelets and knot on back of plaque.

SEASONAL PANELS

Rub edges of a 3 x 2½-inch piece of green handmade paper with brown ink pad.

Cut a 2¾ x 2-inch piece of card stock. Peel backing from a 1½-inch piece of the loop portion of hook-and-loop tape; adhere horizontally to card stock ½ inch from top edge.

Continue to complete individual seasonal designs as instructed below. When all elements are in place, adhere card stock with loop tape to back of seasonal panel with loop tape at top.

CONTINUED on page 119

MATERIALS

- 6-inch-square papier-mâché plaque
- Wheat card stock
- Green handmade paper
- Patterned papers: brown fabric, music and seasonal phrases
- Brown mesh
- Brown corrugated cardboard
- Border rubber stamp
- Alphabet rubber stamps: 9⁄16-inch and ¼-inch
- Solvent-based ink pads: brown and black
- Dye ink: brown and olive
- White acrylic craft paint
- Silk flowers
- Charms: sun, heart and pumpkin
- Winter circle tile
- Decorative fibers
- Green tassel trim
- Fine gold metallic cord
- 2 decorative brass upholstery tacks
- Mini brads: gold and yellow
- Craft knife
- Paintbrush
- Fine sandpaper
- ¾-inch-wide adhesive-backed hook-and-loop tape
- Matte decoupage medium
- Craft glue
- Computer font (optional)

Reaching 50 Tag Book

Design by TANIA WILLIS

Gently tease your favorite "over-the-hill" person with a booklet that tells her all about life at 50. Change the age to suit the recipient!

Use computer or hand print desired quotes and sayings on card stock and/or patterned paper. (See "How You Know You Reached 50," below.) Size 14 fonts work well; to add emphasis to a single word, enlarge it to size 18. Trim around words as desired; adhere to tags.

Build each page on a piece of card stock or paper cut the same size as the shipping tag. Adhere all quotations, fasteners, eyelets, brads, staples, etc., to this layer before affixing it to the tag itself. (The tags will be decorated on both sides; anything like a fastener or brad will show on both sides if you affix it directly to the shipping tag.)

Ink edges of tags on ink pads as desired; repunch holes as needed using a circle punch. Punch holes through the square ends of the completed tags to attach fringes of yarn, fiber or string.

Thread all tag pages onto the book ring; add bows of fiber or ribbon to book ring as desired. ■

SOURCES: Patterned papers from KI Memories, Chatterbox and 7gypsies; stamps from Duncan and Hero Arts.

MATERIALS

- Complementary patterned papers
- Complementary card stocks
- 2⅜ x 4¾-inch shipping tags
- Assorted embellishments: mini brads, tags, alphabet tags, metal-rimmed tags, staples, decorative clips, fasteners, etc.
- Assorted fibers and ribbon
- Ink pads
- ¾-inch book ring
- Circle punches
- Adhesive
- Desired computer fonts (optional)

HOW YOU KNOW YOU REACHED 50

Your arms are too short to read the newspaper.
You no longer think of speed limits as a challenge.
The end of your tie doesn't come anywhere near the top of your pants.
You quit trying to hold your stomach in, no matter who walks into the room.
You can't remember the last time you lay on the floor to watch television.
You have a party and your neighbors don't even realize it.
People call at 9 p.m. and ask, "Did I wake you?"
Your ears are hairier than your head.
You're asleep, but others worry that you're dead.

Birthday Accordion Book

Design by TANIA WILLIS

Tuck a little gift card in each pocket of this unique birthday gift book.

Lay 8½ x 11-inch card stock on work surface with longer edges at top and bottom. Evenly fold up bottom so that edge is ½ inch from top; crease (this will form the pockets). To create accordion folds, fold the folded card stock in half from top to bottom, folding it away from you (back sides facing); crease. Open up (leave pocket strip folded up) and fold each side in until it touches the center crease; crease.

Working from left to right, complete pocket flaps, cutting along creases as needed: First panel, fold down right corner of pocket; second, cut a semicircular notch in the top edge; third, tear top edge at an angle; fourth, fold down pocket edge ¾ inch.

Enhance pockets with staples, stickers, journaling, mini brads and other embellishments as desired. When attaching staples, brads, etc., pierce only the front layer of the pocket.

Close pocket strip, applying adhesive only along outermost edges of first and fourth panels. Before closing the fourth pocket completely, insert the file folder tab so that tab is visible when book is closed.

Cut a piece of card stock to fit in each pocket; punch holes along one edge and decorate with ribbons and fibers. Add journaling, stamped sentiments, stickers and other embellishments as desired. Stamp "celebrate" on card stock; trim to fit in file folder tab and insert in tab.

Cover front and back covers of book with patterned paper. Decorate cover as desired with stickers, beads strung on craft wire, etc. Tie ribbon around book in a bow to hold it closed. ■

SOURCES: Patterned paper from Chatterbox; stickers from Wordsworth; washer and brads from Making Memories; twist-tie from Pebbles Inc.; stamps from Hero Arts; chalk ink pad from Clearsnap.

MATERIALS

- 8½ x 11-inch sheet of card stock for background
- Complementary patterned papers
- Complementary card stocks
- Word and alphabet stickers
- Alphabet stamps
- Ink pads
- Complementary chalks
- Assorted embellishments: staples, mini brads and washers
- Complementary ribbons, fibers and printed twist-ties
- Craft wire
- Seed beads
- Clear file folder tab
- ⅛-inch circle punch
- Fine-tip markers
- Adhesive
- Adhesive dots

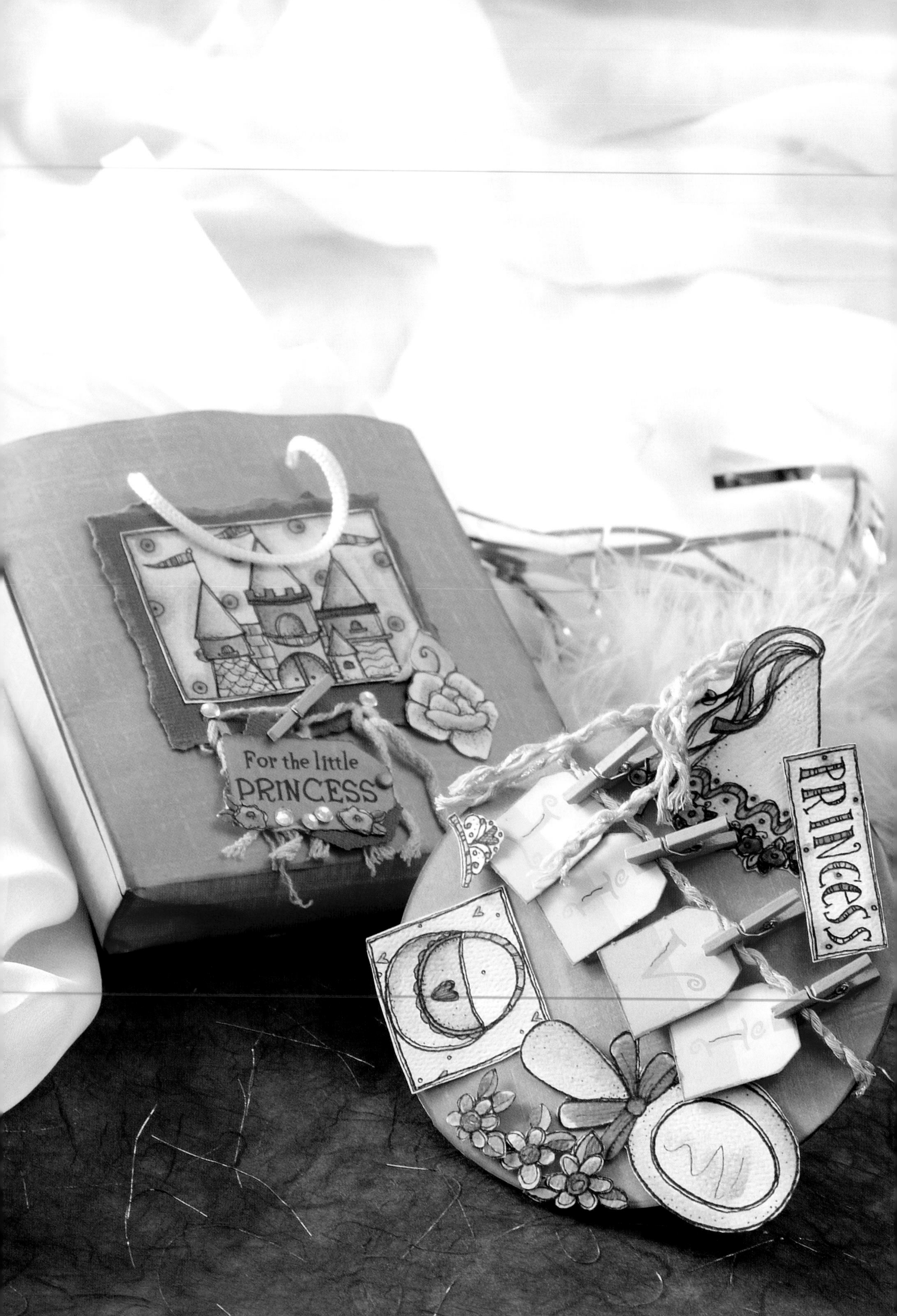

For the little
PRINCESS
PRINCESS

Princess Gift Set

Designs by JEANNE WYNHOFF

This altered CD and coordinating gift bag make a just-right gift for your favorite princess—no matter how old she may be!

Gift Bag

Cut pink patterned paper 12 x 7 inches. Using diagram provided, score ⅝-inch tabs down sides and 1-inch-wide fold across center for bottom of bag; cut center tabs from edge to fold line. Fold center tabs in; fold bag together, overlapping sides; adhere using adhesive squares. Ink edges of bag using purple chalk ink pad.

Punch matching holes in front and back of bag, 1¾ inches apart and 1 inch from top edge. Cut two 6-inch pieces of white cord; thread ends through holes; knot ends inside bag.

Wrap fiber around the lower right corner of the castle cutout; adhere ends on back using adhesive dots. Tear purple card stock 3¼ x 3 inches. Adhere castle cutout to card stock using adhesive squares, positioning cutout toward top.

Punch three holes, evenly spaced, across bottom of purple card stock; the hole farthest to the right should be 2¼ inches from left edge. Cut three 3-inch pieces of fiber. Fold each in half; thread folds through holes from back to front; thread ends through loops and pull snug to create 1½-inch fringes.

Thread a 2-inch piece of fiber across purple card stock through first and last holes; adhere ends on back using adhesive dots. Adhere rhinestones over first and last holes using adhesive dots. Clip clothespin to 2-inch fiber; adhere to card stock using adhesive dots. Adhere purple card stock with cutout to bag using adhesive squares.

Print and punch "For the little PRINCESS" tag from pink patterned paper; ink edges using purple chalk ink pad. Punch another tag from purple card stock. Adhere printed tag to card-stock tag at an angle using adhesive squares. Punch hole through tags; set purple mini brad in hole. Adhere rhinestones and tiny flower cutouts across bottom of tag using adhesive dots. Clip tag in clothespin; adhere tag to gift bag using adhesive foam dots.

Adhere larger rose cutout over lower right corner of purple card stock using adhesive foam dots.

SOURCES: Patterned paper from Provo Craft; paper cutouts from PM Designs; chalk ink pad by Clearsnap; tag punch from Fiskars.

CONTINUED on page 168

MATERIALS

- Pink patterned paper
- Purple textured card stock
- Princess-theme color paper cutouts
- Clear round rhinestones
- Purple mini brad
- 1-inch spring clothespins
- Decorative fibers
- White craft cord
- Purple chalk ink pad
- ⅛-inch circle punch
- 1⅛ x 15/16-inch tag punch
- Adhesive squares
- Adhesive dots
- Adhesive foam dots

Grandparents' Brag Book

Design by TANIA WILLIS

Make it easy for grandparents to show off their collection of photos with this unique photo album!

Remove entire layer of paper from inside of coin holder book. This will expose several layers of cardboard that form the base for holding the coins. Carefully peel away these cardboard layers in one whole piece. Adhere photos and patterned papers directly to the back of this layered cardboard piece.

When all photos and patterned papers are adhered over openings, reposition layered cardboard piece in coin holder book and glue in place.

Add embellishments to openings filled with patterned paper and to the cardboard itself.

Open book and lay it facedown on work surface; measure it as one large piece. Cut width slightly larger than measurement; cut length precisely to size. If desired, using sewing machine to stitch a strip of complementary paper to the base paper using a zigzag stitch.

With book closed, adhere patterned paper first to front cover; wrap paper around to back, and adhere to back cover. *Do not* apply adhesive to spine; this will allow cover to "give" while opening and closing.

Embellish cover as desired. ■

SOURCES: Patterned papers from KI Memories; alphabet rubber stamps from Duncan and Hero Arts.

MATERIALS

- Book-fold or trifold coin holder book for Eisenhower/ Anthony coins
- Complementary patterned papers
- Assorted embellishments: mesh, slide mounts, beads, charms, pins, buttons, stickers, tags, bookplates, silk flowers, etc.
- Assorted alphabet stamps, stickers, tiles, etc.
- Ink pads
- Assorted fibers, string and ribbon
- Photos to fit behind openings in coin holder book
- Craft knife
- Sewing machine and complementary thread (optional)
- Adhesive

Desk Calendar

Design by HEATHER D. WHITE

Each month of this calendar is a personal tribute to family and friends!

Trim 5¼ x 6½-inch sections from desired background layouts to fit on pages facing calendar pages. Rub brown ink pad over edges and surfaces.

Cut patterned paper to fit within background layouts; rub brown ink pad over edges and surfaces. Adhere patterned papers to background layouts using double-sided tape.

Mat photos on patterned paper as desired and adhere to page layouts using double-sided tape. Embellish individual pages with charms, brads, stickers, borders, paper accents, etc.

Stamp names of months across tops of calendar pages using alphabet rubber stamps and brown ink pad. Adhere page layouts opposite calendar pages using double-sided tape. ■

SOURCES: Calendar, papers, border strips, metal stickers, charms, accent bar, mini brads, twill alphabet and stickers from All My Memories; PSX rubber stamps from Duncan.

MATERIALS

- 5½ x 6¾-inch desk calendar with wire binding
- Complementary background layouts and patterned papers
- Complementary paper borders and accents
- Metal accent bar and charms
- Silver mini brads
- Metal stickers
- Twill word stickers
- Silver-trimmed ivory typewriter-key stickers
- Word stickers
- Typewriter alphabet rubber stamps
- Brown ink pad
- Photos
- Craft knife
- Double-sided tape

Family History Box

Design by CARLA JACOBSEN

MATERIALS

- Open-topped box, any shape or pattern, no larger than 12 inches in any dimension
- 12-inch squares of two complementary scrapbooking papers: solid or all-over print, and a larger print
- Printed transparency image
- Card-stock image
- "generations" metal plaque
- 2 yards decorative fiber
- Silk flowers
- Sewing machine with sewing thread
- Decoupage medium
- Hot-glue gun

Create an instant heirloom—a keepsake cache for priceless vintage photos, birth announcements, genealogy information and other family treasures.

Cut pieces of the solid scrapbooking paper to cover bottom half of box, matching patterns and/or color tones where possible; adhere using decoupage medium. Repeat to cover top half of box with second scrapbooking paper, overlapping first layer and trimming along bottom edge to accentuate pattern. At top, fold edges neatly over edge and adhere inside using decoupage medium.

Adhere transparency and card-stock images on front of box using decoupage medium.

For edging around top, cut enough 1¾-inch-wide strips from second scrapbooking paper to fit around top of box. Fold strips in thirds along their length, overlapping sides on back. Machine stitch 2 strands of fiber down the center of each strip using a zigzag stitch. Brush decoupage medium over the front and back of each strip.

Hot glue edging strips around top of box; hot glue silk flower and "generations" metal plaque to front of box. ■

SOURCES: Scrapbooking papers from Creative Imaginations; transparency image and card stock image from Hot Off The Press; metal plaque from Li'l Davis Designs; decoupage medium from Plaid.

Teacher's Sign

Design by SAM COUSINS

Start the school year out right with an adorable door hanger for your child's teacher. A tape measure makes an eye-catching hanger!

MATERIALS

8 x 5-inch papier-mâché panel
Blackboard patterned paper
Library card with red pocket
5½ x 6-inch cork sheet
Alphabet rubber stamps
1½-inch alphabet foam stamps
Black ink pad
Green staples
2 square red metallic brads
Heart-in-hand paper charm
Plastic tape measure
3 silk daisies
Paper glue
Craft cement

Remove rope handle from papier-mâché panel. Cover panel with blackboard patterned paper using paper glue. Adhere tape measure around edges using craft cement; cut off excess and reserve for hanger.

Rub edges of library card and pocket with black ink pad; adhere pocket in lower right quadrant of papier-mâché panel using paper glue. Stamp "SSHHHH CLASS IN PROGRESS" on top of card using alphabet rubber stamps; insert in pocket.

Tear edges of cork sheet; rub edges with ink. Stamp with teacher's name using 1½-inch foam stamps. Attach to bottom of papier-mâché panel using green staples.

Cut hanging loop from remaining tape measure; attach to papier-mâché panel using craft cement. Add square brads over ends of hanging loop; adhere daisies and paper charm using craft cement. ■

SOURCES: Patterned paper from Rusty Pickle; library card and pocket from The Designer's Library; cork sheet from LazerLetterz; PSX rubber stamps from Duncan; stamps and staples from Making Memories; paper charm from Pebbles Inc.

A B C

Teacher's Mini Album

Design by BARBARA GREVE

What teacher wouldn't love this tiny apple album nestled in a nest of crinkled paper?

MATERIALS

Red corrugated paper
Card stock: green and brown
Blue-and-white plaid patterned paper
Plain white paper
Crinkled yellow paper shreds
Paper raffia: yellow, red and green
2½-inch terra-cotta pot
2 (⅛-inch) red eyelets and eyelet-setting tool
3 square silver brads
Square alphabet stickers for brads
Round silver mini brad
Craft paints: yellow and blue
Burgundy embroidery floss
Paintbrush
⅛-inch circle punch
Paper piercer
Large-eye needle
Permanent adhesive
Jewel glue

POT

Paint rim of terra-cotta pot yellow; paint body of pot blue. Let dry. Tie red and yellow raffia in a bow around pot; fill pot with yellow paper shreds.

ALBUM

Fold red corrugated paper in half, smooth side out, with grooves running vertically. Using pattern provided, transfer pattern for outer covers to folded corrugated paper, aligning dashed line with fold; cut out. In the same fashion, transfer pattern for pages/inner covers to folded blue plaid paper; cut out. Use the pattern for pages/inner covers to cut three or four pairs of pages from plain white paper.

Fold red corrugated album cover closed, corrugated side out. Using circle punch, punch matching holes in each edge opposite fold; set eyelets in holes.

Using patterns provided, cut stem from brown card stock and leaf from green. Glue stem to back of front red cover. Using circle punch, punch a hole near top edge of cover, just to left of stem (x on pattern).

Using paper piercer, punch holes in leaf. Using needle and green raffia, stitch leaf through holes, bringing needle up at outer points, one by one, and taking it down through a center hole. Using permanent adhesive, adhere raffia ends to back of leaf. Using circle punch, punch a hole in the base of the leaf. Aligning punched holes in leaf and cover, attach leaf to cover with mini brad.

Transfer alphabet stickers to square brads. Punch holes in front cover; attach brads through holes. Using permanent adhesive, adhere blue plaid inner covers inside red covers.

Open pages and stack with edges even; position inside open cover. Using paper piercer, punch three holes down spine, through pages and cover. Thread needle with 3 strands separated from a length of burgundy embroidery floss; stitch pages and cover together, knotting ends in middle of album. Secure knot with a drop of jewel glue; let dry, then trim ends of floss.

For ties, knot a piece of burgundy embroidery floss (all six strands) in each eyelet. Secure knots with a drop of jewel glue; let dry, then trim. Knot ties again 3¾ inches from eyelets; trim ends. Tie ties in a bow. Nestle album in pot. ■

SOURCES: Plaid paper from Doodlebug Design Inc.; raffia from DMD Inc.; brads and transfers from Creative Imaginations; mini brad and eyelets from Making Memories; adhesives from Beacon.

DRAWINGS on page 167

ADVICE
from
MOM
With

Advice From Mom

Design by RACHAEL GIALLONGO

Even college kids will benefit from this timely advice from Mom, and this fun little book is a great cure for freshman homesickness!

Paint the library pocket using random strokes of blue, yellow and red paints. Adhere a pencils sticker to front; stamp sticker with "Advice from Mom" using desired rubber stamps and black ink pad. Decorate with colored staples.

Cut yellow card stock 4 x 12 inches. Score down the strip at the 3-, 6- and 9-inch positions; fold strip accordion-style. Rub edges on black ink pad.

Decorate panels as desired. Adhere pockets cut from card-stock scraps, or attach card-stock strips using mini brads or heart eyelets. Stamp tags with sayings using blue ink pad; add journaling using pens. Tie fabric strips, ribbon or rickrack through holes in tags. Tuck tags in pockets or under card-stock strips, or adhere to panels. Attach heart charms, stickers, colored staples, etc. Adhere the vellum envelope to the "Call Me!" panel, flap side out; tuck a few coins inside envelope.

Tuck accordion booklet into pocket. ■

SOURCES: Library pocket from Jest Charming Embellishments; stickers from Pebbles Inc

MATERIALS

- Plain library pocket
- Card stock: yellow, plus scraps of blue and red
- 1⅜ x 2¾-inch manila tags
- 2⅛-inch square vellum envelope
- Pencil stickers
- Acrylic craft paints: red, yellow and blue
- Alphabet rubber stamps
- Ink pads: black solvent-based and blue
- Stapler with color staples
- Mini brads
- Heart eyelets
- Scraps of fabric, ribbons, rickrack, etc.
- Fine-tip felt pens or gel pens
- Paintbrush
- Paper glue
- Craft cement

Bookmark Trio

Designs by SAHILY GONZALEZ

Add a personalized bookmark to the latest best seller for a thoughtful gift.

"Read" Bookmark

Cut a 6¼ x 3⅛-inch strip of card stock; cover with patterned papers as desired using glue stick. Rub edges of bookmark on sand dye ink pad. Adhere narrow strips of mesh along edges of bookmark.

Using alphabet stamps and black ink pad, stamp "Read" in center of bookmark; add "a book that makes you happy" below it using a fine-tip marker. Adhere metal corners on either side of "Read" using craft cement; paint corners with pink paint and rub off excess. Brush edges of bookmark and mesh with pink paint.

In upper left corner, write "When I'm attacked by gloomy thoughts, nothing helps me so much as running to my books. They quickly absorb me and banish the clouds from my mind. —Michel de Montaigne."

Punch a ¼-inch hole in center top of bookmark; thread fibers through hole. Punch ⅛-inch hole near upper right corner. Separate two layers of petals from fabric flower; attach to card stock by attaching the pink mini brad through the center of the flower. Adhere "B" sticker below and to left of flower. ■

SOURCES: Patterned papers from K&Company; adhesive mesh from Magic Mesh; decorative corners from Making Memories.

MATERIALS

- Craft card stock
- Patterned papers
- Natural adhesive mesh
- Decorative fibers
- Metal corners
- Pink mini brad
- Round "B" sticker
- Alphabet rubber stamps
- Black ink pad
- Sand dye ink pad
- Pink acrylic craft paint
- Black fine-tip marker
- Pink fabric flower
- Circle punches: ⅛-inch and ¼-inch
- Small paintbrush
- Glue stick
- Craft cement

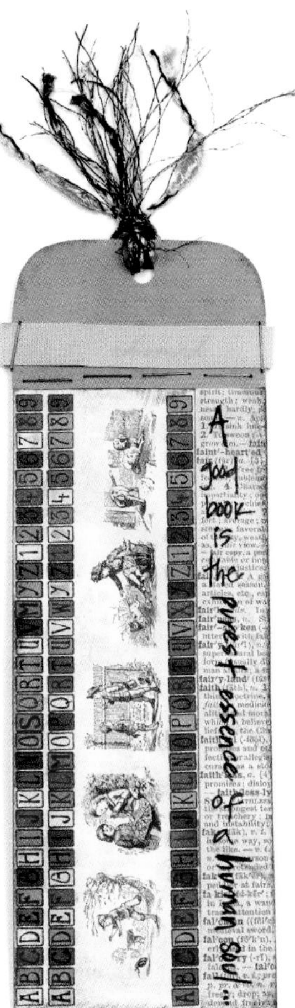

Alphabet Bookmark

MATERIALS

Tan suede card stock
Patterned papers
Suede paper
⅜-inch-wide pale blue imprinted ribbon
Decorative fibers
Sepia dye ink pad
Black fine-tip marker
¼-inch circle punch
Glue stick

Cut card stock to desired size for bookmark; cover with patterned papers and suede paper as desired using glue stick. Rub edges of bookmark over sepia dye ink pad.

By hand, write "A good book is the purest essence of the human soul" down side of bookmark using black fine-tip marker.

Staple a length of imprinted ribbon across top of bookmark; add more staples as desired. Punch hole in top of bookmark; thread decorative fibers through holes. ■

SOURCES: Patterned papers from 7gypsies.

Purple & Green Bookmark

Cut a 6 x 3¼-inch strip of lavender card stock; cover with patterned papers as desired using glue stick. Add a 1¾-inch "file folder tab" along the right edge. Rub edges of bookmark over sand dye ink pad.

By hand, write "Only books have the ability to simultaneously shut out the world and open it up. … Laura Bush" on bookmark using black fine-tip marker.

Staple imprinted transparency across center of bookmark. Punch holes along top of bookmark; set green and lavender brads in holes, wrapping decorative fibers around brads.

Separate two layers from sheer green organza flower; attach to card stock by attaching the decorative brad through the center of the flowers. Adhere epoxy sticker to tab. ■

SOURCES: Patterned papers, transparency strip and epoxy sticker from Creative Imaginations; brads from Making Memories.

MATERIALS

Patterned papers
Lavender card stock
Brads: lavender, green and brass decorative
Epoxy "books" sticker
Imprinted transparency strip
Assorted ribbons and decorative fibers
Sand dye ink pad
Black fine-tip marker
Sheer pale green organza flower
¼-inch circle punch
Stapler with staples
Glue stick

Back to School Clipboard

Design by SAM COUSINS

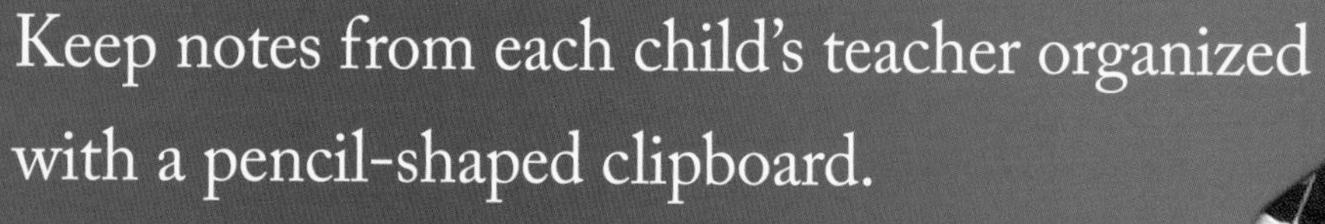

Keep notes from each child's teacher organized with a pencil-shaped clipboard.

Project note: *Adhere elements using paper glue unless otherwise instructed.*

Wrinkle red paper; evenly crease yellow paper lengthwise. Smooth out both pieces. Adhere blackboard patterned paper to tip of pencil. Adhere yellow paper to body of pencil, tearing edge adjacent to blackboard paper. Adhere red paper over eraser area. Trim off excess paper using a craft knife.

Adhere a triangle of silver tape to very tip of pencil for lead; adhere a 1-inch-wide strip of tape to separate eraser from pencil. Adhere a 3⅞ x ⅞-inch strip of metal mesh over the 1-inch strip of tape.

Adhere spring clips along bottom of pencil using heavy-duty adhesive. Stamp names around clips.

Rub black ink pad over wrinkles and creases in red and yellow papers, and over edges of pencil. Adhere stickers to pencil to spell "SCHOOL STUFF." ■

SOURCES: Patterned and decorative papers from Rusty Pickle, Karen Foster Design and Paper Fever Inc.; metal mesh from Making Memories; stickers from Sticker Studio; PSX stamps from Duncan.

MATERIALS

3⅞ x 14¼-inch wooden pencil plaque
Decorative papers: yellow and red
Blackboard patterned paper
Silver metal mesh
1½-inch alphabet stickers
Silver electrical tape
¼-inch alphabet rubber stamps
Black ink
Magnet-backed metal spring clips
Craft knife
Sawtooth hanger
Paper glue
Heavy-duty adhesive

Recipe Card Magnet

CONTINUED FROM PAGE 99

Rub twill tape on brown liquid chalk ink pad; adhere across front of folder near bottom using adhesive dots; wrap ends around to inside and adhere using adhesive dots.

Tear squares of brown and tan card stock to mat photos; rub edges on brown liquid chalk ink pad. Mat photos on card stock squares, arranging them on the diagonal; adhere to front of file folder using adhesive dots. Add candy bar and "yum" stickers and punch-outs to front of folder using adhesive dots. Slide a paper clip over front flap of folder on right-hand edge.

Use computer or hand print a favorite chocolate recipe on tan card stock using brown ink so that recipe fits within a 4⅛ x 5¼-inch area. Trim around recipe, trimming top edge in the shape of a recipe card with tab. Rub edges of card with brown liquid ink pad. Adhere stickers to tab and upper right corner of card; coat exposed sticky areas with chalk.

Adhere recipe card inside folder, letting it hang out over the top at an angle. Inside folder, adhere "sweet" sticker below recipe; adhere candy bar punch-out just below fold using adhesive dots and covering ends of twill tape. Close folder; secure with a paper clip.

Hot glue laminate chips together, lining up the holes but overlapping them at an angle. Thread 6 inches of fiber through holes. Adhere folder with recipe card to laminate chips using adhesive dots and squares and positioning holes on right side. Adhere magnets on back of chips. ■

SOURCES: Stickers and punch-outs from Creative Imaginations; chalk ink pad from Clearsnap.

Seasonal Wall Plaque

CONTINUED FROM PAGE 101

Summer panel: Stamp "SUMMER SUN" down left side using ¼-inch alphabet stamps and black ink pad. Poke gold mini brads through centers of silk flowers in summer colors; attach up right side. Wrap decorative fiber across bottom; secure on front and back using dots of craft glue. String sun charm on gold cord and knot to hold charm in place; wrap gold cord across bottom and secure ends on back with craft glue.

Autumn panel: Adhere a ¾ x 2½-inch strip of autumn seasonal phrases paper across bottom. Poke gold mini brads through centers of silk flowers in autumn colors; attach to panel. Suspend a pumpkin charm from flower in upper left corner using decorative fiber.

Winter panel: Adhere a ¾ x 2½-inch strip of winter seasonal phrases paper across bottom. Poke gold mini brads through centers of burgundy and white silk flowers; attach to upper right corner. Adhere a winter circle tile using craft glue.

Spring panel: Adhere a ¾ x 2½-inch strip of spring seasonal phrases paper across bottom. Poke yellow mini brads through centers of silk flowers in spring colors; attach to panel. Suspend a heart charm from flower in upper left corner using gold cord. ■

SOURCES: Handmade paper and fabric patterned paper from Creative Imaginations; music patterned paper from Rusty Pickle; seasonal phrases patterned papers from Pressed Petals; brown mesh from Magenta; border stamp from Stampabilities; alphabet stamps from Hero Arts and Rubber Stamp Ave.; solvent-based ink pads from Tsukineko Inc.; matte decoupage medium from Golden Artist Colors.

October Through December

As fall turns to winter, there are so many reasons to celebrate and give unexpected gifts. Choose your favorite projects and create several for drop-in guests!

CARDS
SUPPLIES
ALOHA
give thanks

HAPPY HAUNTING
SPOOKY
Try Some
BLACK BAT
LICORICE
Magic Potions
candy
candy
candy

Happy Haunting Magnet

Design by SUSAN STRINGFELLOW

Conjure a wonderfully spooky magnet with stickers of vintage paintings and a tiny magic-potion bottle complete with fairy dust!

Project note: *Adhere papers to CD using liquid adhesive; adhere other elements using paper glaze.*

Thoroughly sand both sides of CD so that glue will adhere. Trace around CD onto back of brown patterned card stock; cut out using a craft knife and adhere to front of CD using liquid adhesive.

Tear a 1½ x 5-inch strip of ivory card stock. Dampen it, crumple it, smooth it out and allow to dry. Rub brown ink over surface. Adhere to right edge of CD.

Crumple edges of haunted house image; decoupage it onto left side of CD using matte medium. Apply three coats of matte medium over image; let dry.

Adhere a ½ x 5-inch strip of dotted mesh across bottom of CD onto ivory card stock; dry-brush gold paint around edges of haunted house and edges of CD. Randomly stamp decorative image onto CD using foam stamp and gold paint.

Stamp "SPOOKY" over haunted house and "HAPPY HAUNTING" along top edge of CD using alphabet stamps and black ink. Adhere black-cat image at an angle over crumpled ivory card stock using dots of paper glaze. Tie a small bow of black ribbon; adhere near upper left edge of black-cat image.

Crumple "Black Bat Licorice" image; smooth out and mat on orange patterned paper, adhering with paper glaze. Sand edges of orange patterned paper; rub edges with black ink pad. Adhere image to lower portion of CD using adhesive dots.

Pour gold glitter into bottle; glue cork in place using paper glaze. Tie ribbon in a bow around neck of bottle. Use computer or hand print "Magic Potions $1" on ivory card stock to fit within a ⅜ x 1¾-inch rectangle. Trim card stock to size; poke a hole in left end using a needle; thread gold cord through hole and tie tag to bottle. Adhere bottle to right of licorice image using paper glaze.

Adhere magnet strips or dots to back of CD. ■

SOURCES: Patterned card stock from Paper Loft; patterned paper from Pixie Press; self-adhesive mesh from Magic Mesh; vintage images from Altered Pages; foam stamps from Making Memories; stamps from Rubber Stamp Ave.; solvent-based ink from Tsukineko Inc.; decoupage medium from Golden Artist Colors; liquid adhesive from Tombow; paper glaze from JudiKins.

MATERIALS

- CD
- Card stock: patterned brown and solid ivory
- Orange patterned paper
- Self-adhesive mesh
- Vintage images: black cat, haunted house and "Licorice"
- Decorative foam stamps
- ¼-inch alphabet stamps
- Ink pads: brown and black
- ⅜-inch-wide sheer black ribbon
- 1-inch glass ink bottle
- Ultrafine gold glitter
- Gold metallic acrylic craft paint
- Fine gold cord
- Fine sandpaper
- Craft knife
- Needle
- Paintbrushes
- Magnet strips or circles
- Computer font (optional)
- Adhesive dots
- Matte medium
- Paper glaze
- Liquid adhesive

MATERIALS

- CD
- Patterned paper: yellow and orange
- Purple mulberry card stock
- Green reversible card stock
- Black "dotted" self-adhesive mesh
- Paper Halloween kitty image
- White polymer clay
- 2 purple bat buttons
- ½-inch purple round button
- Orange embroidery floss or thread
- Decorative fibers
- Metal witch hat and moon charms
- Silver metal swirl clip
- "Boo to You" rubber stamp
- Tiny alphabet rubber stamps
- Speckled background stamp
- Multicolored ink pad
- Black ink pad
- Fine sandpaper
- Craft knife
- Acrylic brayer or roller
- Paper towels
- Magnet circles or strips
- Liquid adhesive
- Paper glaze

Boo to You Magnet

Design by SUSAN STRINGFELLOW

Helpful Halloween characters add a touch of whimsy while keeping notes secure on a refrigerator or filing cabinet.

Project note: *Adhere papers to CD using liquid adhesive; adhere other elements using paper glaze.*

Sand surface of CD so that adhesive will adhere. Adhere yellow patterned paper to cover bottom 1 inch of CD; adhere a 2-inch strip of purple mulberry card stock to cover left side of CD; adhere a 4-inch square of orange patterned paper to cover upper right area of CD.

Trim paper and card-stock edges even with CD. Stamp entire surface of disk using speckle stamp and black ink pad. Adhere a 5 x 1-inch strip of paper mesh across bottom half of CD.

Rub edges of kitty image on black ink pad. Sand edges of a 1½ x 2½-inch rectangle of green card stock; rub edges on black ink pad. Adhere kitty to green rectangle at an angle; fold up lower right corner of card stock; adhere. Thread orange floss through purple flat button; adhere to folded corner. Clip silver clip over upper edge; adhere entire piece to CD on left side, overhanging edge slightly.

Using brayer, roll polymer clay ⅛ inch thick. Stamp "Boo to You" in clay; trim a 1¼ x 3½-inch oval around words. Punch a hole in each end of oval; bake stamped clay and let cool. Rub surface randomly with green, yellow, purple and orange inks, wiping off excess. Thread six 6-inch lengths of fiber through each hole; knot. Adhere clay tile to CD.

Rub edges of hat and moon charms on black ink pad; adhere to CD. Adhere bat buttons in upper right corner. Using alphabet stamps and black ink, stamp "candy" randomly over surface.

Adhere magnet dots or strips to back of CD. ■

SOURCES: Adhesive mesh from Magic Mesh; kitty image from PM Designs; rubber stamps from Close to My Heart and Hero Arts; multicolored ink pad from Clearsnap; solvent-based ink pad from Tsukineko Inc.; liquid adhesive from Tombow; paper glaze from JudiKins.

Alien Halloween Card

Design by LORETTA MATEIK

All's well—this alien only came for the chocolate! Give these fun cards to all the neighborhood trick-or-treaters!

Fold a 9¼ x 8-inch piece of orange card stock in half to form a 9¼ x 4-inch card with fold on left edge. Adhere a 7⅛ x 3¾-inch rectangle of black card stock near bottom of card using glue stick.

Adhere alien die cut to black card stock using glue stick; adhere candy bar between alien's hands, using adhesive foam dots to hold arms in place.

Use computer or hand print "Relax … I'm only here for the candy!" on lime green card stock to fit within a 1½ x 2¾-inch rectangle. Trim card stock to size; adhere to top of card using adhesive foam dots. ■

SOURCES: Die cut from Designs by Loretta.

MATERIALS

- Card stock: orange, black and lime green
- Business-size envelope
- Green paper alien die cut
- Miniature candy bar
- Glue stick
- Adhesive foam dots
- Computer font (optional)

Halloween Joke Book

Design by CARLA JACOBSEN

Tickle the funny bones of anyone who appreciates a good laugh at silly jokes! Create enough of these books to give out at class parties!

COVERS

Cut two pieces of cardboard 3¼ x 4¾ inches; punch hole in upper left-hand corner of each. Paint covers with two coats black paint, then one coat of decoupage medium.

Cut orange card stock 2½ x 3½ inches; adhere irregular stripes cut from yellow, purple and black card stock. Use computer or hand print "HALLOWEEN BOOK" on orange card stock; cut out letters and adhere to striped panel. Use computer or hand print "joke" on yellow card stock; trim to fit behind acrylic bookplate, then run card stock through sticker maker backwards so it will stick to back of bookplate. Use paper piercer to poke holes through cover where bookplate will be attached, but do not attach it yet.

Coat striped panel with decoupage medium; when dry, stitch bookplate to panel using needle and black thread. Adhere panel to front cover at an angle. Run skull and bones through sticker maker; adhere to cover. Paint cover with decoupage medium, avoiding acrylic bookplate.

PAGES

Cut six pages of card stock 3¼ x 4¾ inches; punch hole in upper left-hand corner of each. Use computer or hand print jokes on different colors of card-stock; trim and adhere to card-stock pages. (See the sidebar for sample jokes; the Internet is another source.)

Embellish pages as desired: Adhere stripes and punched circles of contrasting card stock; machine stitch around some jokes; set eyelets in some pages. Vary colors, positions and embellishments.

Sand flat end of screw post; paint black. Coat with decoupage medium. Assemble pages and covers on screw post with painted end on front. If screw post is too long for thickness of book, tie decorative fibers around the post between some pages to expand the book to fill the post. ■

SOURCES: Card stock, laser cuts and acrylic bookplate from DMD Inc.; decoupage medium from Plaid; sticker maker and repositionable adhesive cartridge from Xyron.

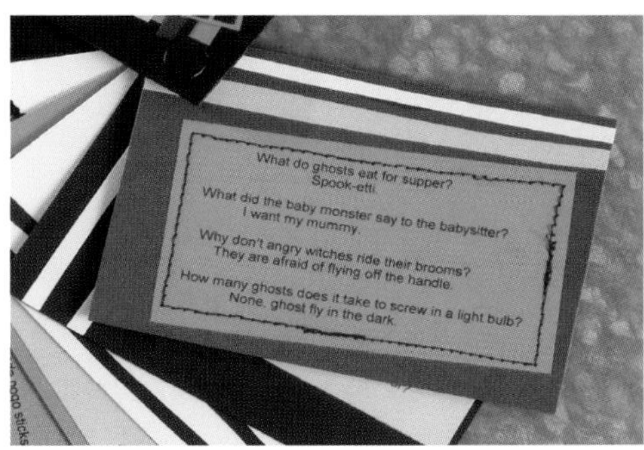

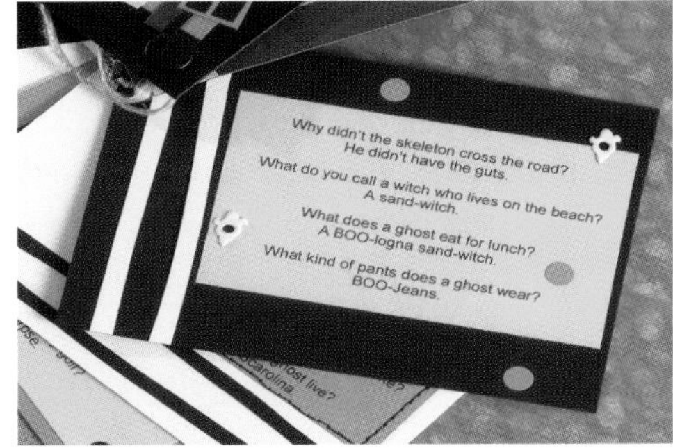

HALLOWEEN JOKES

What do ghosts eat for supper?
Spook-etti.

What did the baby monster say to the baby-sitter?
"I want my mummy."

Why don't angry witches ride their brooms?
They are afraid of flying off the handle.

How many ghosts does it take to screw in a light bulb?
None; ghosts fly in the dark.

Why didn't the skeleton cross the road?
He didn't have the guts.

What do you call a witch who lives on the beach?
A sand-witch.

What does a ghost eat for lunch?
A BOO-logna sand-witch.

What kind of pants does a ghost wear?
BOO-jeans.

What is a ghost's favorite fruit?
BOO-berries.

What do witches put on their hair?
Scare-spray.

What kind of mistakes do ghosts make?
Boo-boos.

Where do most ghosts live?
In North Scarolina.

What kind of shoes do baby ghosts wear?
Boo-ties.

Why did Dracula drink cold medicine?
To stop his coffin.

What is a ghost's favorite bedtime story?
"Little Boo Peep."

Where do ghosts play golf?
A golf corpse.

What do witches eat at Halloween?
Spooketti, Halloweenies, devil's food cake and booberry pie.

What did the really ugly man do for a living?
He posed for Halloween masks.

Why didn't the skeleton go to the party?
He had no body to go with.

What happened when the skeletons rode pogo sticks?
They had a rattling good time.

Why did the skeleton go to the hospital?
To have his ghoul stones removed.

What's a skeleton's favorite musical instrument?
A trom-bone.

MATERIALS

- Thin, stiff cardboard
- Card stock: black, yellow, orange, purple and white
- Laser-cut skull and bones
- Acrylic bookplate
- Round, ghost and bat eyelets and eyelet-setting tool
- Black acrylic craft paint
- Decorative fibers
- Sticker maker with repositionable-adhesive cartridge
- ¼-inch circle punch
- Paintbrush
- ⅜-inch metal screw post
- Paper piercer or large needle
- Fine sandpaper
- Sewing needle
- Sewing machine with black sewing thread
- Jokes
- Decoupage medium
- Liquid adhesive
- Computer fonts (optional)

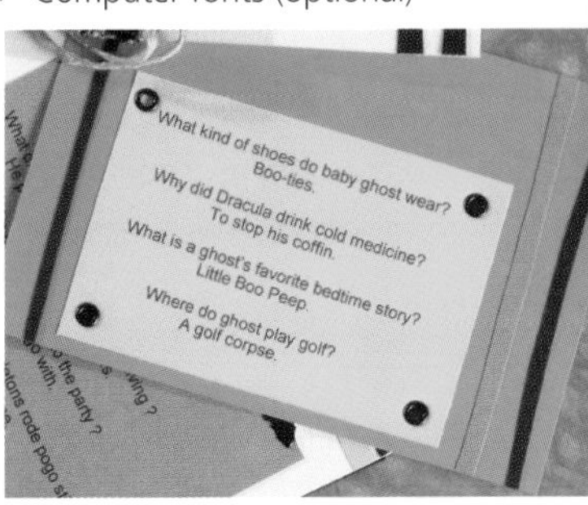

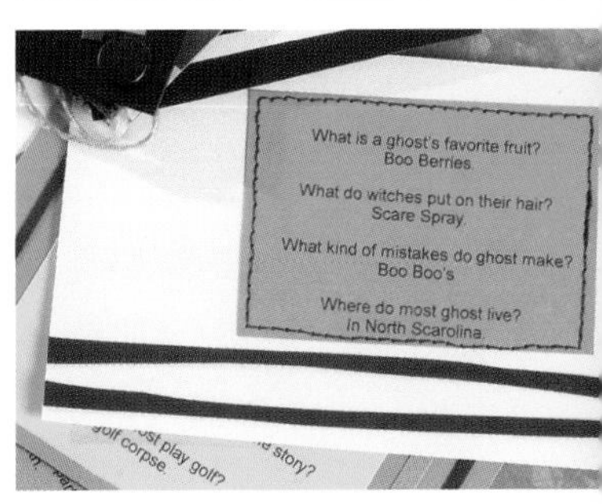

Monster Treat Boxes

Designs by MARY AYRES

Altered matchboxes become frightfully fun treat boxes by adding card stock and simple embellishments.

Cut an 8½ x 4¾-inch piece of purple paper; wrap around matchbox, creasing at corners, but do not adhere.

Adhere two ¼-inch circles of black card stock to two ½-inch circles of yellow card stock for eyes. Punch one ½-inch circle from orange card stock for nose; adhere eyes and nose to rectangle of purple paper that will be on top of matchbox.

Below nose, punch a pair of ⅛-inch holes ½ inch apart and ¾ inch from left edge of purple paper; add another pair of ⅛-inch holes ¾ inch from right edge. Set eyelets in holes. String black burlap through holes and knot at each end for mouth; trim burlap ends to ½ inch. Adhere decorated paper around matchbox.

Cut two 1⅜ x 2½-inch rectangles from neutral paper; adhere to ends of matchbox.

Knot together several strands of green raffia; adhere at center top of face for hair. Tie three strands of natural burlap into a bow; adhere under mouth toward right side.

Transfer a Halloween rub-on transfer onto neutral paper; tear rectangle around words, leaving room to punch hole. Rub edges of tag on orange ink pad. Punch ⅛ inch hole in tag; set eyelet in hole. Thread black burlap strand through eyelet; tie around hair. Adhere tag to hair.

Repeat to make a second monster treat box, substituting green paper for purple and purple raffia for green. ■

SOURCES: Rub-on transfers from Royal & Langnickel; adhesive from Beacon.

MATERIALS

- 2 (2½ x 4¾ x 1½-inch) cardboard matchboxes
- Card stock: orange, yellow and back
- Tone-on-tone papers: green, purple and neutral
- Orange ink pad
- Halloween rub-on transfers
- 10 (⅛-inch) round copper eyelets and eyelet-setting tool
- Raffia: green and purple
- Strands pulled from burlap fabric: black and natural
- Circle punches: ½-inch, ¼-inch and ⅛-inch
- Permanent adhesive

Halloween Mini Crate

Design by KATHLEEN PANEITZ

Fill this little crate with all sorts of Halloween treats for neighborhood ghosts and goblins!

Cut two 1¼ x 2⅜-inch rectangles from textured orange card stock and one from black card stock. Rub edges of orange rectangles on black dye ink pad; rub edges of black rectangle on white pigment ink pad. Center and adhere rectangles on tags.

Punch a hole in the center of each end of each tag; set orange eyelets in holes in black tag and black eyelets in holes in orange tags.

Thread ribbon inside crate, over top edge of crate and through bottom slit. Thread bottom end of ribbon through eyelet at bottom of black tag; bring it up through eyelet at top of black tag. Tie ribbon ends in a bow at top of black tag, positioning it in center on side of crate. Repeat to attach orange tags to crate on each side of black tag.

Snap shanks off buttons using wire cutters; adhere ghost button to black tag; adhere witch button and spider to orange tags. ■

SOURCES: Tags from Making Memories; buttons from Jesse James & Co. Inc.

MATERIALS

- Textured orange card stock
- Black card stock
- 3¾ x 5¾ x 4⅛-inch wooden crate
- 3 (1½ x 2⅝-inch) tags with metal rims
- 1¼-inch Halloween buttons: witch and ghost
- 1½-inch rubber spider
- Orange and black eyelets and eyelet-setting tool
- Black dye ink pad
- White pigment ink pad
- ¼-inch-wide black-and-white gingham ribbon
- ⅛-inch circle punch
- Wire cutters
- Craft glue

Boo Door Hanger

Design by SAM COUSINS

Grandma will love this Halloween card that doubles as a door hanger. It features a cute ghost created by stamping a child's foot!

Cut patterned paper to desired size (sample measures 6¼ x 5½ inches). Tear another piece from a complementary pattern to overlay the first. Adhere both sheets on black card stock, sandwiching a strip of mesh between the patterned papers down right edge; tear edges of card stock. Rub torn edges on white chalk ink pad. Secure layers using green staples.

Brush the bottom of your child's foot with white paint; have him "stamp" his foot on black card stock. (Heel will be head of ghost; toes will be bottom.) Trim around image; use black fine-tip marker to note name and age along edge, and to draw eye circles and wires for glasses. Adhere ⅜-inch domed stickers over eyes. Tie ribbon in a bow around ghost's neck; adhere ghost to background.

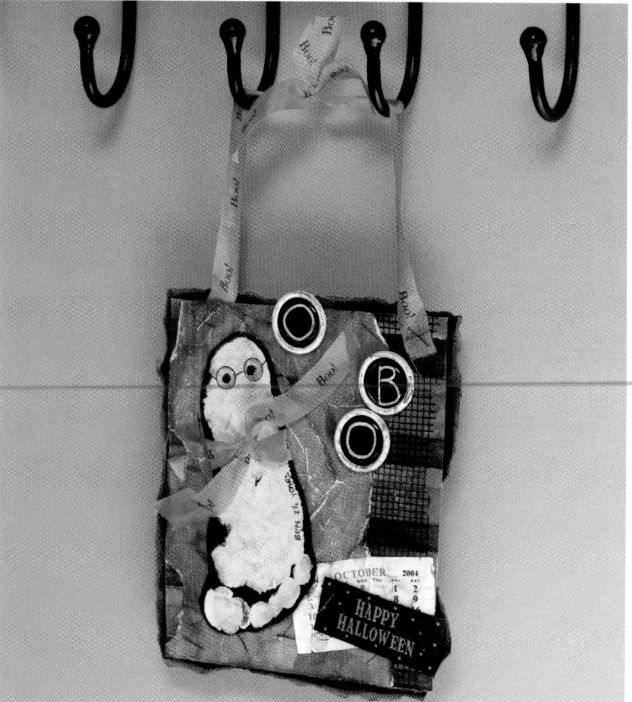

Paint frame fasteners green; when paint is dry, scratch most of it off. Mount frame fasteners over letters to spell "Boo"; top each letter with a ¾-inch domed sticker. Adhere letters to door hanger.

Crumple calendar page; smooth out and adhere in lower right corner. Using green staples, affix fabric Halloween label over calendar page, leaving 31 visible; adhere a ⅜-inch domed sticker over 31. Use green staples to attach ribbon for hanging loop. ■

SOURCES: Patterned papers from Rusty Pickle; ribbon from Impress Rubber Stamps; frame fasteners from Scrapworks; domed stickers, green staples and paints from Making Memories; letters from Doodlebug Design Inc.; fabric label from Me & My Big Ideas; chalk ink pad from Clearsnap.

MATERIALS

- Complementary patterned papers in Halloween colors
- Black card stock
- October page torn from small calendar
- Black adhesive mesh
- Orange "boo!" ribbon
- 1-inch white alphabet cutouts or stickers
- 1-inch round white frame fasteners
- Green staples
- Clear domed stickers: ⅜-inch and ¾-inch
- Fabric "Happy Halloween" label
- Craft paints: green and white
- White chalk ink pad
- Black fine-tip pen
- Craft glue

Thanksgiving Recipe Book

Design by HEATHER D. WHITE

Create a special album to hold cherished family recipes. Present this gift to newlywed couple or to college graduates moving into their first home!

Cut patterned paper 4¼ x 5½ inches for front cover. Tear a piece of contrasting paper to fit along bottom; cut a triangle to fit in upper left-hand corner. Adhere papers. Embellish cover with stickers as desired. Lightly sand edges and surfaces of cover.

Use computer or hand print individual recipes on patterned papers to fit on 4¼ x 5½-inch pages, leaving room at top and bottom to add embellishments.

Trim pages to size; lightly sand edges and surfaces of all pages. Embellish pages as desired using stickers, tags attached with eyelets, brads, etc. (If a recipe completely fills a page, do not crowd it by adding embellishments.)

Back each completed page with a 4¼ x 5½-inch piece of patterned paper. Sand edges and surfaces on backs of pages.

Punch matching holes in the top left corner of each page; set eyelets in holes. Stack pages and thread fibers through holes to tie together. Knot fibers, leaving fiber ends rather long, and leaving enough "play" so that pages slide open and closed easily. ■

SOURCES: Patterned papers and stickers from Pebbles Inc.

MATERIALS

- "Antique" patterned papers
- Antique-style alphabet stickers
- Paper label and tag stickers: travel, family and fall themes
- Neutral decorative fibers
- ⅛-inch round black eyelets and eyelet-setting tool
- Brads
- Fine sandpaper
- ⅛-inch circle punch
- Double-sided tape
- Computer font (optional)

Giving Thanks Box

Designs by KATHY LEWIS

Place a special tag inside the box for each member of your family. Throughout the year, have them write down special things they're thankful for to take out and read on Thanksgiving day!

BOX

Adhere pieces torn from four or five patterned papers to outer and inner surfaces of box using decoupage medium; overlap pieces for a collaged look. Rub chalk ink pads over box edges and randomly over surfaces.

Stamp background images on box using dye ink pad; adhere quote sticker inside lid. Tear the edges of doors image; adhere to lid at an angle on right side. Dry-brush over edges of picture using a complementary craft paint for an aged appearance. Coat entire box with a thin layer of decoupage medium.

Paint bookplate; thread fibers through holes and adhere fibers and bookplate using adhesive dots. Transfer or stamp "giving" on card stock; trim to fit in bookplate; insert. Stamp or transfer "thanks" onto lid.

Clip stems off silk flowers and leaves; adhere blossoms and leaves using craft cement. Paint paper glaze onto lid along lower left corner of doors image and elsewhere as desired; quickly apply gold microbeads. Adhere coordinating button in lower right corner of doors image using craft cement. Tie fibers to old key; adhere key across top of box using craft cement.

Poke hole in center of lid ½ inch from front edge using an awl. Cut a 2¼ x ½-inch piece from the hook portion of the hook-and-loop tape; tack to the box lid through the hole using needle and strong thread. Cover hook portion of tape with decorative ribbon. Cut a small piece from the loop portion of the hook-and-loop tape; adhere to side of box using craft cement.

Wrap wire-edge ribbon around the box, tying a bow on the front.

TAGS

Rub edges of the library pockets on chalk ink pads. Using patterned papers, alphabet stickers, fibers, rubber stamps and other embellishments, create a pocket to represent each family member. Choose favorite colors and other embellishments to reflect individual personalities.

For each pocket, cut a 4 x 2-inch tag from complementary card stock; rub edges over an ink pad. Loop fibers through the hole; tuck tag in pocket. Add journaling to tags—special memories, things for which to be thankful, etc. Place pockets with tags in the box to share on Thanksgiving Day or another special time. ■

SOURCES: Patterned papers from Chatterbox, NRN Designs and Provo Craft; library pockets and doors image from Altered Pages; rubber stamps from Stampers Anonymous and A Stamp In the Hand; chalk ink pads from Cleasnap; microbeads and paper glaze from JudiKins; decoupage medium from Plaid; craft cement from Eclectic Products Inc.

MATERIALS

- Pencil or cigar box
- Patterned papers
- Doors paper image
- Library pockets
- Card stock
- Decorative fibers, fringe and buttons
- Wire-edge 1 5/16-inch-wide ribbon
- Silk flowers and leaves
- Metal bookplate
- Quote stickers
- Rubber stamps: background images and alphabet
- Chalk ink pads
- Dye ink pads
- Acrylic craft paints
- "Giving" and "thanks" rubber stamps or rub-on transfers
- Gold microbeads
- Old key
- Additional embellishments for individual tag pockets: twill tape, word beads, mosaic squares, label maker with tape, decorative paper clips, brads and fasteners
- Hook-and-loop strip
- Paintbrushes
- Wire cutters
- Awl
- Sewing needle and strong thread
- Fine-tip markers or gel pens
- Decoupage medium
- Paper glaze
- Craft cement
- Adhesive dots

Fall Patchwork Frame

Design by SANDRA GRAHAM SMITH

Embossing powder makes the stamped leaves on this frame glow with all the brilliance of autumn trees.

From each color of card stock, cut several 1½-inch-long strips wide enough to cover frame. Alternating colors, adhere strips to frame using double-sided adhesive.

Cut three or four 1½-inch squares from each color of card stock. Stamp a leaf onto each square using embossing ink pad; sprinkle with embossing powder and emboss.

Adhere embossed card-stock squares to frame, spacing them evenly and aligning outer edges of squares with outer edges of frame. (Squares will overhang center opening somewhat.) ■

SOURCES: Card stock from DieCuts with a View; stamp from Northwoods Rubber Stamps.

MATERIALS

- 8½ x 6⅝-inch flat frame with 7 x 5-inch opening
- Textured card stock: brown, green, rust and dark gold
- Leaf rubber stamps
- Clear embossing ink
- Copper embossing powder
- Embossing heat gun
- Double-sided adhesive

Thanksgiving Favors

Designs by RENAE CURTZ, COURTESY OF STAMPIN' UP

Add a special personal touch to your Thanksgiving feast with a stamped treat bag for each guest.

FAVOR BAGS

Stamp image on white card stock using black ink; enhance using colors painted from remaining ink pads. Cut out; center and adhere to a 1½-inch square of complementary card stock using adhesive-backed foam square.

Wrap hemp cord around the center of a tag, or adhere a strip of mesh across the center. Adhere stamped image over cord or mesh using adhesive-backed foam squares.

Stamp "give thanks" or other lettering in bottom right corner of tag; embellish as desired using mini brads.

Fill cellophane bag with trail mix. Punch hole in top of tag; thread hemp cord through hole and tie around neck of bag to close; or, thread hemp cord through a button before threading it through the tag and tying it around the neck of the bag.

FAVOR BOXES

Cut a 1½ x 2½-inch rectangle of card stock. Tear the left-hand edge so tag measures 2¼ inches wide; roughen the torn edge by running a scissors blade over it.

Stamp nature image on white card stock using black ink; enhance using colors painted from the remaining ink pads. Cut out; adhere onto the right-hand side of the card stock using adhesive-backed foam square. Wrap hemp cord around card stock; knot on front.

Center and adhere card stock to the copper tag using adhesive-backed foam squares; bend up lower left corner of copper tag. Adhere copper tag to front of assembled gable box using adhesive-backed foam squares.

Fill box with trail mix; close box. Thread hemp cord through a complementary button; knot ends on front; adhere button to center top flap using craft glue. ■

SOURCES: Card stock, box, tag sheets, buttons, stamp sets, ink pads, twine, adhesive mesh, brads, tags, cellophane bags and adhesive-backed squares from Stampin' Up!

MATERIALS

- Card stock: white, red, olive green and brown
- 2⅞ x 1½-inch card stock tags
- Small cellophane bag
- Gable box
- 1⅜-inch square nature images rubber stamps
- Alphabet rubber stamps
- Ink pads: black, red, brown, caramel brown, olive green and mustard yellow
- Fine hemp cord
- Natural adhesive-backed mesh
- Antique-finish mini brads
- ⅜-inch flat buttons
- 1¼ x 2½-inch copper metal tag
- Trail mix, snack mix, etc.
- ⅛-inch circle punch
- Paintbrush
- Adhesive-backed foam squares
- Nontoxic craft glue

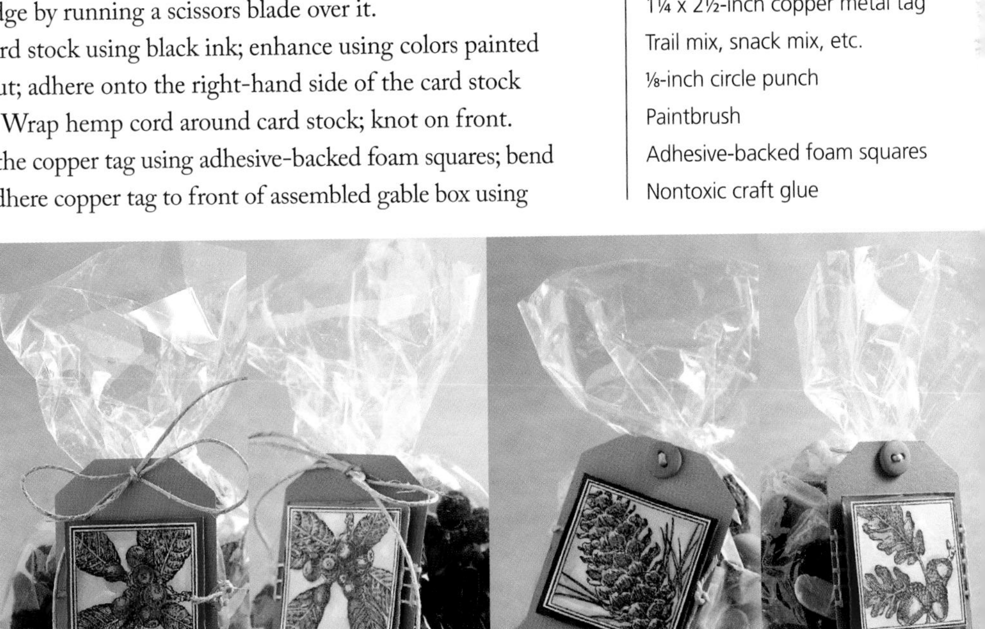

Fall Leaf Candle Wraps

Design by CHERYL BALL, COURTESY OF DUNCAN ENTERPRISES

Metallic papers and leaf stamps create beautiful candle wraps that will be a hit at your Thanksgiving feast.

Stamp a topaz maple leaf on gold card stock or evergreen patterned paper; sprinkle with clear embossing powder and emboss. Repeat to make four or five leaves for each candleholder, stamping leaves in a variety of colors on both metallic gold paper and evergreen patterned paper, and embossing with clear or gold embossing powder.

Cut out the leaves, leaving a narrow border of background paper showing. Use a push pin to poke a hole in the base of each leaf and at the end of each vein. Cut a small piece of gold or copper wire; poke one end through the tip of a vein and bend end flat on back of leaf. Poke the other end through the hole in the base of the leaf; bend the end flat on the back. Repeat to add wire veins to each leaf.

Using craft cement, glue a coordinating stone bead at the base of each leaf, covering the hole. Let dry.

Cut a strip of natural mulberry paper to fit around candleholder with 1-inch overlap. Tear along the long edges; apply permanent adhesive to both ends of strip and glue strip around candleholder. Tie brown ribbon around candleholder over paper strip; knot on front. Secure with a dot of permanent adhesive under knot and at center back. Cut olive green ribbon to fit around candleholder; glue in place. Trim ribbon ends.

Cut a 12-inch piece of gold cord. Tie it around the brown knot. Loop the gold cord back and forth to make bow loops; lay loops over knot and tie cord ends to secure. Trim and knot ends of cord.

Adhere leaves to candleholder using foam mounting squares. ■

SOURCES: PSX evergreen patterned paper, mulberry paper, rubber stamps, embossing powder, mounting squares, and cement from Duncan; permanent adhesive from Tombow.

MATERIALS

- Evergreen patterned paper
- Natural mulberry paper
- Metallic gold card stock
- Glass candleholder
- Maple leaf rubber stamp
- Pigment ink pads: topaz, paprika and evergreen
- Embossing powder: gold and clear
- 1½ yards brown organza ribbon
- 1 yard ½-inch-wide olive green ribbon
- 3 yards metallic gold cord
- 24-gauge wire: copper and gold
- Complementary stone beads
- Craft cement
- Embossing heat gun
- Push pin
- Wire cutters
- Permanent adhesive
- Foam mounting squares

Ornament & Pine Branch Plaques

Design by MARY AYRES

Brightly colored stamped pine branches are striking when placed on colorful card stock and plaques.

PINK PLAQUE

Lightly sand plaque. Paint center panel white. Paint edges light pink. Dry-brush edges using gold metallic paint.

Adhere masking tape to white center panel along edges, keeping tape straight. Adhere two more rows of tape next to the first, butting edges and keeping tape straight. Peel off the center row of tape and sponge exposed areas using gold metallic paint, painting squares in the corners as shown.

Stamp a pine branch onto light green card stock using gold ink pad; cut out and adhere to upper right corner of plaque using adhesive dots.

Using pattern provided, cut an ornament circle from bright pink card stock. Cut a 1½ x 3½-inch strip from light pink card stock. Stamp border on strip using gold ink pad; trim long edges using decorative-edge scissors. Adhere strip to ornament; trim ends to match edges of ornament. Rub edges of ornament on gold ink pad; lightly spray ornament using glitter spray.

For ornament cap, cut a ¾ x 1½-inch rectangle from gold corrugated paper; trim one long (bottom) edge with decorative-edge scissors. Fold strip in half; glue to top of ornament using instant-dry paper glue.

Punch hole in top of ornament cap. Bend a 2½-inch piece of wire into a 1⅝-inch ornament hook; thread end through hole in ornament cap and twist. Adhere ornament and cap to plaque using adhesive dots.

PEACH & PURPLE PLAQUES

Repeat instructions for pink plaque, substituting peach and purple paints and card stocks for pink. ■

SOURCES: Wooden plaques from Walnut Hollow; rubber stamps from Hero Arts and All Night Media/Plaid; glitter spray from Krylon; Zip Dry paper glue from Beacon.

DRAWINGS on page 169

MATERIALS

- 3 (5 x 7-inch) unfinished wooden plaques
- Card stock: white, light pink, bright pink, light orange, bright orange, light purple, bright purple and light green
- Gold metallic corrugated paper
- 28-gauge gold craft wire
- Border rubber stamp
- Pine branch rubber stamp
- Gold ink pad
- Multicolor glitter spray
- Acrylic craft paints: white, light peach, pink, light purple and metallic gold
- ¼-inch-wide masking tape
- 1/16-inch circle punch
- Decorative-edge scissors
- Paintbrushes
- Craft sponge
- Fine sandpaper
- Adhesive dots
- Instant-dry paper glue

Christmas Holly Leaf Jar

Design by MARY AYRES

Pretty enough that it doesn't need wrapping, this jar is the right size to fill with cookie ingredients or hot chocolate mix.

Spray jar lid with stone-finish gold paint.

Cut a 3½-inch square from gold tone-on-tone paper; tear a 4-inch square from red suede paper. Center and adhere gold square to red suede square. Using sewing machine and gold thread, zigzag around gold square.

Using patterns provided, cut three holly leaves from green card stock and two from olive green card stock; rub edges with gold ink pad. Cut one branch from brown card stock; rub edge along underside with brown ink pad. Punch five ¼-inch berries from red card stock. Adhere leaves, branch and berries to gold paper square.

CONTINUED on page 169

MATERIALS

- Card stock: green, olive, red and brown
- Gold tone-on-tone patterned paper
- Plain vellum
- Red suede paper
- Glass quart jar with lid
- 3 (⅛-inch) round gold eyelets and eyelet-setting tool
- 2 mini round gold brads
- ½-inch-wide red-and-white checked ribbon
- ⅝-inch-wide green-and-white striped ribbon
- Stone-finish gold metallic spray paint
- Ink pads: gold and brown
- Circle punches: ¹⁄₁₆-inch, ⅛-inch and ¼-inch
- Sewing machine and gold thread
- Computer fonts (optional)
- Permanent adhesive

Happy Holidays Tin

Design by PARIS DUKES, COURTESY OF HOT OFF THE PRESS

Send a photo CD or make a CD of favorite Christmas music and enclose it in this tin for a special gift for a faraway friend or family member.

Wipe lid of CD tin with lemon juice or vinegar. Trace lid onto back of red patterned paper; tear around circle so that it is slightly smaller than lid. Adhere red patterned paper to lid using collage medium and foam brush.

Tear or cut paper images; adhere to red background using decoupage medium. Cover slide mount with green patterned paper using collage medium; cut out opening using craft knife. Mount "Happy Holidays" artwork behind slide mount. Punch three holes, evenly spaced, down right side of slide mount; thread burgundy and black ribbons through holes; knot and trim ends. Adhere slide mount to CD case using foam tape.

Adhere label tape phrases to background using collage medium. Knot short lengths of black ribbon; trim ends and adhere next to label tape phrases using decoupage medium. ■

SOURCES: CD tin, background papers, paper art, collage medium, slide mount, ribbon and paper phrases from Hot Off The Press.

MATERIALS

CD tin
Red and green Christmas patterned papers
Christmas paper art
Large square slide mount
⅜-inch-wide grosgrain ribbons: black and burgundy
Paper holiday "label tape" phrases
Foam brush
¼-inch circle punch
Craft knife
Lemon juice or vinegar
Decoupage medium
Foam tape

Christmas Gift Tag

Design by RACHAEL GIALLONGO

Favorite family photos are a great way to create a very personal tag for holiday gifts!

MATERIALS

- Card stock: dark green and light green
- 1⅝ x 2-inch light green enameled tile
- Alphabet rubber stamps
- Black solvent-based ink pad
- Self-adhesive red 4-inch zipper
- ½-inch red-and-white gingham ribbon
- ⅛-inch round red eyelets and eyelet-setting tool
- ⅛-inch circle punch
- Christmas photo
- Sewing machine and white thread
- Glue stick
- Adhesive foam dots

Cut a 7¾ x 4¼-inch tag from dark green card stock. Using a glue stick, mat the photo on top portion of tag, leaving a ⅛-inch-wide border. Cut a pocket from light green card stock for bottom of tag, again trimming to leave a ⅛-inch-wide border. Machine stitch the light green pocket to tag down sides and across bottom. Adhere zipper over seam between photo and pocket.

Punch a hole in center top of tag; set eyelet in hole; thread gingham ribbon through hole. Using alphabet stamps and black ink pad, stamp "happy holidays" on the tile. Thread gingham ribbon through the hole in tile; adhere tile in center of light green pocket using adhesive foam dots.

Cut small tags from light green card stock; punch holes in end and set eyelets in holes. Using alphabet stamps and black ink pad, stamp "to" and "from" on tags. Add names; tuck tags into zippered pocket. ■

SOURCES: Tile and zipper from Junkitz; PSX alphabet stamps from Duncan; solvent-based ink pad from Tsukineko Inc.

Golden Star Bag

Design by SANDRA GRAHAM SMITH

Metallic stars add instant glitz to a simple gift bag, making a classy gift presentation.

Using die-cutting machine and embossing plate, make two stars from gold metallic card stock; cut out, leaving ⅛-inch border.

Using pattern provided, cut two stars from blue card stock; adhere to front of bag. Center and adhere gold stars to blue stars.

Form a 1½-inch-square gift tag from blue card stock; punch hole in corner. Adhere two stickers to front of bag and one to gift tag. Thread gold thread through hole in tag; tie to handle of bag. ■

SOURCES: Stickers from Stampendous; die-cutting machine and embossing plate from Sizzix/Ellison.

DRAWINGS on page 170

MATERIALS

- Card stock: dark blue and gold metallic
- 8½ x 5¼ x 3⅛-inch white paper bag with handles
- Gold metallic thread
- "Merry Christmas" stickers
- Die-cutting machine
- Star embossing plate
- Small circle punch
- Glue stick

Seasons Greeting Card

Design by HARRIET VICK, COURTESY OF CLEARSNAP

Add dimension and shine to this season's greeting card with a square tile and embossing ink. The tile removes to become a seasonal pin.

Using the inking brush, apply green ink to recessed areas of tree and lined background on Christmas tree tile; use opposite end of brush to apply yellow gold color to recessed stars. Wipe off excess. Heat-set inks using embossing heat tool; let cool. Tap the tile onto the red ink pad to ink raised areas; heat-set and let cool. Ink the sides of the tile with the yellow-gold ink; heat-set and let cool.

Apply yellow ink to white card stock; apply green ink to another piece of white card stock. From the yellow piece cut 1½-inch square and a piece 1¼ x 2¾ inches; from green piece cut a 1¾-inch square and a piece 1½ x 3 inches. From a scrap of red glittery card stock, cut a piece 1 x 2½ inches.

Using green ink, stamp "Season's Greetings" on red rectangle; center and adhere on yellow rectangle; center and adhere on green rectangle. Adhere rectangles to bottom of card using glue stick.

Center and adhere yellow square on green square; adhere squares near top of card using glue stick. Center and adhere Christmas tree tile on yellow card-stock square using tacky double-sided tape. ■

SOURCES: Card stock from Yellow Rose Art Stamps; faux stone tile, inking brush and ColorBox MicaMagic ink pads from Clearsnap.

MATERIALS

- Red glittery card stock
- White card stock
- Faux carved stone tile: Christmas tree
- "Season's Greetings" rubber stamp
- Ink pads: green, red and yellow gold pearlized
- Inking brush
- Embossing heat tool
- Craft knife
- Tacky double-sided tape
- Glue stick

Snowman Styles Card

Design by HARRIET VICK, COURTESY OF CLEARSNAP

Send a cute snowman card to friends and family throughout the winter months as a "just because" greeting. The surprise gift? The snowman is part of a removable bracelet!

BRACELET

Using the inking brush, apply silver ink to recessed areas of snowman and three snowflake tiles; wipe off excess. Tap tiles onto blue ink pad; heat set to dry ink. Tap edges of tiles on silver ink pad; heat set and let cool. Gently tap each tile on white ink pad for a very light touch of color; heat set and let cool.

String tiles and beads on a 12-inch length of silver 24-gauge wire, saving third snowflake tile for last. String both ends of wire through holes in third snowflake tile and trim to 1 inch. Thread a small silver bead on each end; coil wires to hold in place.

Thread a 6-inch piece of silver wire through bottom holes in snowman tile; add a bead to each end and coil. Adhere an adhesive foam square to back of top snowflake tile and snowman tile; set aside.

CARD

Fold an 11 x 5½-inch piece of blue sparkle card stock in half to form 5½-inch-square card. Randomly stamp snowflakes over 5-inch silver vellum square using silver, blue and white ink pads. Heat set to dry ink. Center and adhere stamped vellum on front of card using glue stick.

Adhere bracelet to front of card using adhesive foam squares. Remove bracelet by carefully peeling it off the adhesive foam squares. ■

SOURCES: Card stock from Yellow Rose Art Stamps; carved stones, inking brush, ColorBox MicaMagic ink pads, Crafter's Ink Pad and stamp from Clearsnap.

MATERIALS

- Blue glittery card stock
- Silver vellum
- Faux carved stone tiles: snowman and snowflakes
- Snowflake rubber stamp
- Ink pads: blue and silver pearlized; white pigment
- 24-gauge silver wire
- Silver and blue beads
- Inking brush
- Embossing heat tool
- Wire cutters
- Needle-nose pliers
- Adhesive foam squares
- Glue stick

Christmas Boxes

Designs by KATHLEEN PANEITZ

Cover papier-mâché boxes in your favorite printed paper to create a package that is as much fun as the gift it contains!

Square Box

Cover box and lid with red patterned paper using decoupage medium. When dry, coat box and lid with decoupage medium; let dry completely.

Cut an oval of olive green patterned paper to cover front of oval tin tile; adhere using craft glue. Stitching through paper, stitch through holes around tin tile using needle and gold metallic thread. Adhere oval Christmas tile in center of oval tin tile using craft glue; adhere oval tin tile in center of box side using craft glue.

Tie sheer olive ribbon around box, tying ends in a bow on top of lid. ■

SOURCES: Patterned papers from Magenta and Mustard Moon; tin tile from Making Memories; oval metal tile from K&Company; decoupage medium from Back Street Inc.

MATERIALS

- Square papier-mâché box with lid
- Red and olive green patterned papers
- Oval stitched tin tile
- Oval metal Christmas-art tile
- 15/16-inch-wide sheer olive green ribbon
- Fine gold metallic thread
- Sewing needle
- Decoupage medium
- Craft glue

Round Box

Cover box sides and lid with complementary patterned papers using decoupage medium. Cover bottom of box with the same paper used to cover lid, and adhere a strip of that same paper around bottom edge of box to mimic lid edge. When dry, coat box and lid with decoupage medium; let dry completely.

Leaving a 4-inch tail and beginning on center front of box, adhere red ribbon around box over seam where papers meet; do not tie or cut ribbon ends, but form them into 1½-inch bow loops and secure in center using craft glue. Trim excess ribbon.

Adhere foam squares on back of paper Christmas tree accent; position and adhere on box over center of ribbon loops. ■

SOURCES: Patterned papers and tree accent from Kangaroo & Joey; decoupage medium from Back Street Inc.

MATERIALS

- Round papier-mâché box with lid
- Patterned papers
- Paper Christmas tree accent
- 3/8-inch-wide red grosgrain ribbon
- Decoupage medium
- Adhesive foam squares
- Craft glue

Holly Leaf Votive Wrap

Design by SHARON REINHART

Create festive lighting for your holiday event with this elegant votive wrap.

Stamp two holly leaves onto gold vellum using embossing ink; sprinkle with embossing powder and emboss. Repeat to stamp and emboss two holly leaves and two gift bows on olive green paper. Cut out embossed images.

Gently curl tips of holly leaves over the edge of a scissors blade. Adhere leaves to back of one gift bow using adhesive dots, arranging gold leaves on the top and olive green leaves on the bottom.

On remaining gift bow image, lightly crease bow loops along each side of center of bow; adhere on top of first bow using adhesive foam dots.

Cut a 2-inch-wide strip of gold vellum long enough to fit around votive candleholder with ½-inch overlap; trim ¼ inch from each long edge using decorative-edge scissors. Adhere strip around votive candleholder using adhesive dots. Adhere holly-and-bow piece over seam using adhesive dots. ■

SOURCES: Rubber stamps from DeNami Designs and Delta/Rubber Stampede.

MATERIALS

- Olive green iridescent paper
- Gold vellum
- Glass votive holder with candle
- Rubber stamps: holly leaf and bow
- Clear embossing ink
- Gold embossing powder
- Decorative-edge scissors
- Embossing heat tool
- Adhesive dots
- Adhesive foam dots

Christmas Candleholder Trio

Designs by SANDY ROLLINGER

Embellish ceramic candle bases with clay motifs embellished with beads and sparkling fiber!

Spray each candleholder with gesso; repeat as needed. Spray with three light coats of silver spray paint.

Use brayer to roll modeling compound ⅛ inch thick on glass surface. Use cookie cutters to cut one of each shape from modeling compound; let dry. Brush shapes with laminating liquid; sprinkle with glitter and let dry.

For each candleholder, cut a 3-inch-wide strip of handmade silver paper long enough to fit around candleholder. Tear strip along long edges; glue around candleholder with instant-dry paper glue.

Cut a 1½-inch-wide strip of blue mulberry paper long enough to fit around candleholder. Use a paintbrush to apply water to long edges; carefully tear along edges, then glue around candleholder in center of silver paper strip.

Wrap silver braid ribbon around candleholder three or four times in the center of the blue mulberry paper strip; knot ends on front and trim. Cut a 6-inch piece of silver braid ribbon; thread beads onto ends and knot ends. Fold beaded braid ribbon in half; glue fold to knot on candleholder. Glue a paper clay shape over the knot. ■

SOURCES: Air-dry modeling compound from Creative Paperclay Co.; gesso spray and spray paint from Krylon; Liquid Laminate and Zip Dry instant-dry paper glue from Beacon.

MATERIALS

- White air-dry modeling compound
- Handmade silver paper
- Dark blue mulberry paper
- 3 (5-inch-tall) ceramic candle pillars
- Spray gesso
- Silver spray paint
- Silver braid ribbon
- Round and oval beads: blue, black and silver
- Pastel blue ultrafine glitter
- 2-inch cookie cutters: star, tree and snowflake
- Paintbrushes
- Acrylic brayer or roller
- Glass cutting surface
- Laminating liquid
- Instant-dry paper glue

St. Nick Ornament

Design by SANDY ROLLINGER

This jolly fellow is created over a plastic-foam egg. Spiral paper punches create the illusion of a curly beard!

Set the lid open side up on waxed paper. Using a craft stick, coat half of the plastic-foam egg with foam finish; rest it on the lid, coated side up, until dry. Coat other half of egg with foam finish; let dry.

Roll a marble-size ball of modeling compound for pompom; set aside. Using the acrylic brayer, roll a small piece of modeling compound ⅛ inch thick; using star cutter, cut star from modeling compound. Roll a ⅞-inch rounded teardrop for nose. Let dry.

Tear red tissue paper into 1-inch pieces. Using a paintbrush and decoupage medium, cover 1¾ inches at narrow end of egg with red tissue paper. Set egg on lid to dry.

Cut a 2-inch circle of pink tissue paper in half. Using a paintbrush, apply decoupage medium to the foam ball just under the red area. Press half of the pink tissue paper onto the wet medium for face; let dry. Using a paintbrush and decoupage medium, cover the teardrop nose with pink tissue; let dry.

Punch spirals from white card stock. Using decoupage medium, adhere spirals around face and entire large end of egg. Adhere two more spirals to face for mustache. Using instant-dry paper glue, adhere nose over mustache and white pompom to tip of hat. Coat entire egg with decoupage medium; let dry.

For hat brim, cut a ½-inch wide strip of white card stock long enough to fit around egg plus ¼ inch. Run strip through crimper; using instant-dry paper glue, adhere around base of hat.

Paint entire egg pearl white; paint star gold. Using instant-dry paper glue, adhere star to hat brim.

Using instant-dry paper glue, glue hanging loop of fine gold thread around pompom. Add two dots of blue paint to face for eyes. ■

SOURCES: Air-dry modeling compound from Creative Paperclay Co.; Foam Finish, Liquid Laminate decoupage medium and Zip Dry instant-dry paper glue from Beacon; metallic paints from Jacquard Products; paper paint from Plaid.

MATERIALS

- White air-dry modeling compound
- 4-inch plastic-foam egg
- Tissue paper: red and pink
- White card stock
- Foam finish
- Metallic paints: pearl white and gold metallic
- Light blue paper paint
- Fine gold metallic thread
- Paintbrushes
- Spiral punch
- Paper crimper
- Small star clay cutter
- Craft stick
- Small lid
- Acrylic brayer or roller
- Waxed paper
- Decoupage medium
- Instant-dry paper glue

Christmas Elegance Ornaments

Designs by SANDY ROLLINGER

Glass ornaments are painted and covered with paper and glitter to create delicate, shimmering ornaments that will add sophistication to any Christmas tree!

MATERIALS

- Blue mulberry paper
- Silver metallic paper
- 2 (4-inch) clear glass or plastic teardrop ornaments
- Silver metallic paint
- Silver braid ribbon
- Small clear rhinestone stars
- 4mm round white pearls
- Fine crystal glitter
- Paper punches: star and snowflake
- Paintbrushes
- Toothpicks
- Laminating liquid
- Clear-drying glue

BLUE ORNAMENT

Paint ornament caps with silver paint; let dry.

Punch stars from silver metallic paper. Using a ¼-inch flat brush and laminating liquid, cover ornament with small pieces torn from blue mulberry paper; let dry. Using brush and laminating liquid, glue silver stars to ornament.

Wrap silver braid ribbon around ornament between stars, beginning and ending at top. Using a toothpick, apply dots of glue randomly under braid ribbon and at the ends to hold it in place. Using a toothpick, apply dots of glue to ornament between stars; press rhinestone stars into glue. Let dry.

Add a hanging loop of silver braid ribbon to ornament cap.

GLITTER ORNAMENT

Paint ornament caps with silver paint; let dry.

Punch snowflakes from silver metallic paper. Using a ¼-inch flat brush and laminating liquid, glue snowflakes to ornament; let dry. Brush laminating liquid over entire ornament, then sprinkle with glitter; let dry.

Using a toothpick, apply dots of glue to ornament between snowflakes; press pearls into glue. Let dry.

Add a hanging loop of silver braid ribbon to ornament cap. ■

SOURCES: Metallic paint from Jacquard Products; Liquid Laminate and Glass, Metal & More glue from Beacon.

Vintage Images

Designs by SUSAN HUBER

Recycle favorite holiday images between glass slides and surround the edges with solder or metallic foil. These little ornaments are just the right size for a small tree!

Lay slide over desired image; trace around slide and cut out image using craft knife. Cut a matching piece of patterned card stock.

Sandwich card stock and image between two glass slides. Center edges of glass slides on copper tape. Work tape around slides to enclose all edges, keeping tape borders as even as possible. Burnish all surfaces of tape using a bone folder.

Apply flux to copper tape. ***Note:*** *Use flux sparingly, but remember: Solder will only adhere to copper tape to which flux has been applied.* Preheat soldering iron. When hot, heat solder so that it melts, and glide the solder over the copper tape to create a smooth soldered edge all around slides. ***Note:*** *Do not overwork solder or you will not have smooth sides.*

Adhere a jump ring at each end of ornament: Place flux on ring, then attach ring to end of slide with a small drop of solder.

Transfer a Christmas sentiment to plain side of ornament using rub-on transfers. Thread decorative fiber or ribbon through top jump ring for hanger; suspend an ornament or charm from bottom jump ring. ■

SOURCES: Card stock from Memories Complete; glass slides from American Scientific Surplus; rub-on transfers and ornaments from Making Memories, Queen & Co. and Lasting Memories; flux, solder and copper tape from Scrap a Latte.

MATERIALS

- Patterned card stock
- Vintage Santa images
- Glass slides
- Jump rings
- Word rub-on transfers
- Metal charms, tags and ornaments
- Decorative fibers
- Flux*
- Solder*
- Soldering iron*
- Copper tape*
- Craft knife
- Bone folder
- Pliers
- Clamp

*Adhesive copper foil tape can be substituted for soldering materials.

White Poinsettia Frame

Design by SANDY ROLLINGER

Simple quilled flowers create a very elegant frame suitable for treasured photos or family portraits!

Project notes: *Glue ends of quilled paper strips with paper glue to secure individual shapes. Use paper glue to glue quilled shapes and strips to frame and to each other. Use tweezers to position shapes and hold them in place until glue sets. Use craft cement to attach buttons and pearls.*

Using a piece of sea sponge, apply white pearl paint to frame; let dry. In the same manner, apply gold paint to frame; let dry. In the same manner, apply clear gloss finish; let dry.

Cut 28 (4-inch) strips of olive green quilling paper. Using patterns provided, form 13 strips into triangles; form 15 strips into marquis shapes. Cut 29 (4-inch) strips of off-white quilling paper; form each into a marquis shape.

Cut two 9-inch strips and seven 6-inch strips of olive green quilling paper. Form each into a curled stem, curling one end three or four turns to form a circle, and leaving the other end straight.

Cut eight 3-inch strips of olive green quilling paper. Form each into a spiral: Curl quilling paper onto slotted tool in a tight circle. Carefully pull free end off the tool, leaving the other end in the slot. Then pull spiral off slotted end.

Referring to the placement guide for the bottom layer, adhere the long stems to frame; add smaller stems. Adhere olive green and off-white marquis shapes (positions of olive green shapes are indicated by "G"). Adhere olive green triangles along stems. Adhere spirals between marquis shapes.

Referring to pattern for poinsettia top layer, adhere remaining off-white marquis shapes on top of first layer, alternating positions of petals. Adhere a pearl cluster button in center of each poinsettia. Adhere 4mm pearls in clusters of three to triangle leaves. ■

SOURCES: Metallic paints from Jacquard Products; Paper-Tac paper glue and Glass, Metal & More glue from Beacon.

DRAWINGS on page 170

MATERIALS

- ⅛-inch-wide paper quilling strips: off-white and olive green
- Flat 7-inch-square wooden frame with 3-inch square opening
- 3 (½-inch) pearl-cluster shank buttons
- 4mm white pearls
- Metallic paints: white pearl and gold
- Slotted quilling tool
- Sea sponge
- Toothpicks
- Tweezers
- Clear gloss spray finish
- Paper glue
- Craft cement

PARADISE
MELE KALIKIMAKA
CARDS
SUPPLIES
ALOHA
ALOHA
SONGS of HAWAII
PARADISE

Mele Kalikimaka Set

Designs by SUSAN STRINGFELLOW

Celebrate Christmas Hawaiian-style with a two-tier box filled with coordinating cards and a matching pencil.

Project note: *Use matte decoupage medium as adhesive unless otherwise instructed.*

STATIONERY BOX

Remove metal nameplates from box. Cover sides of bottom tier of the box with striped card stock. Cover sides of top tier with pink patterned card stock. Cover lid with floral patterned card stock. Rub all edges of box and lid with brown ink pad. Repunch holes for metal nameplates with awl.

Lightly sand metal nameplates; paint with two shades of green paint. Rub edges lightly with brown ink pad; sand lightly. Separate four layers of petals from silk flowers; poke mini brads through centers; reattach metal nameplates with mini brads.

Sand edges of floral tag; rub edges with brown ink pad. Stamp "Mele Kalikimaka" ("Merry Christmas" in Hawaiian) on tag with alphabet stamps and black ink pad. Fold two 6-inch lengths of ribbon in half; thread folds through hole on right edge of tag; thread ribbon ends through loop and pull snug. Repeat to attach two 16-inch lengths of ribbon through hole on left edge of tag; 1 inch from tag, tie ribbon ends in a bow. Poke a hole in top of box lid near front right corner with awl; poke a hole through ribbon bow and attach to lid using a brad.

STATIONERY

For each of four cards, score a 6 x 12-inch piece of ivory card stock down center and fold to create a 6-inch square card. Center and adhere a 5½-inch square of floral patterned card stock on front of card.

Lightly sand the edges of a vintage image; rub lightly with brown ink pad. Mat image on green bamboo vellum; punch holes in corners with awl and insert mini brads. Overlap a 4-inch strip of mesh and matted image on front of card; adhere with double-sided tape, concealing tape behind image.

Adhere a ¾ x 6-inch strip of striped card stock across top of each envelope flap. Stamp "ALOHA" on right end of strip with alphabet stamps and black ink pad.

PENCIL

Sand pencil. Adhere a 6 x 1-inch strip of floral patterned card stock around pencil with fast-drying craft glue. Rub lightly with brown ink pad.

Tie an 8-inch piece of ribbon around top of pencil. Separate a layer of petals from a small silk flower; poke mini brad through center. Adhere flower to top of pencil with paper glaze. ■

SOURCES: Box from Walnut Hollow; patterned card stock and floral tag from Basic Grey; vellum from Golden Oaks; natural mesh and Hawaiian images from Altered Pages; alphabet stamps from Rubber Stamp Avenue; matte decoupage medium from Golden Artist Colors; paper glaze from JudiKins.

MATERIALS

- 2-tier papier-mâché organizer box
- Patterned card stock: floral, pink and striped
- Floral print tag
- Ivory card stock
- Green bamboo vellum
- Vintage Hawaiian images
- 6-inch-square envelopes
- Pencil
- Natural color mesh
- Small silk flowers
- Light green mini brads
- Complementary ribbons
- Complementary green acrylic craft paints
- Alphabet rubber stamps
- Ink pads: brown and black
- Double-sided tape
- Paintbrushes
- Fine sandpaper
- Awl
- Sponge
- Matte decoupage medium
- Fast-drying craft glue
- Paper glaze

Groundhog Day Frame

CONTINUED FROM PAGE 17

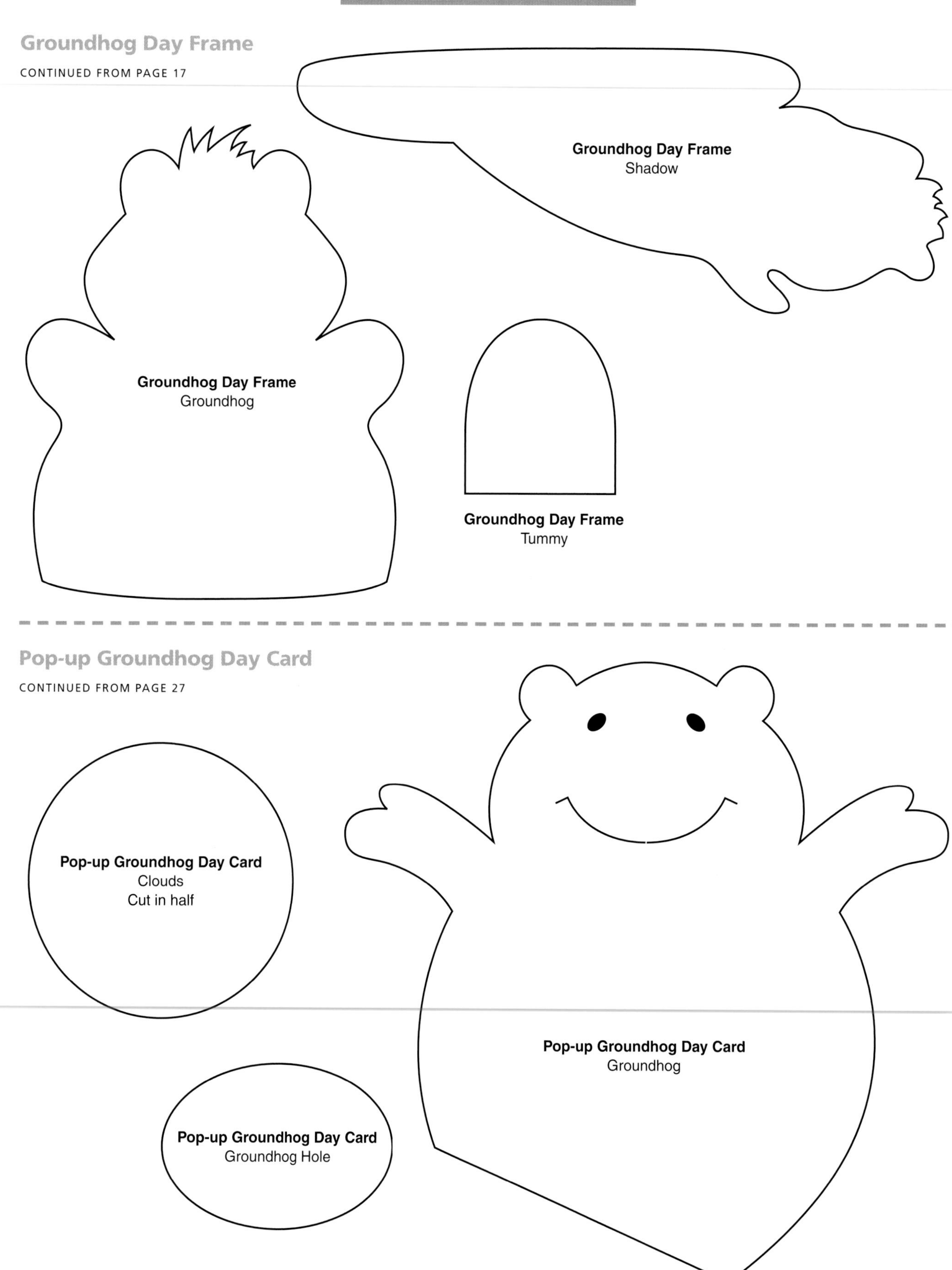

Pop-up Groundhog Day Card

CONTINUED FROM PAGE 27

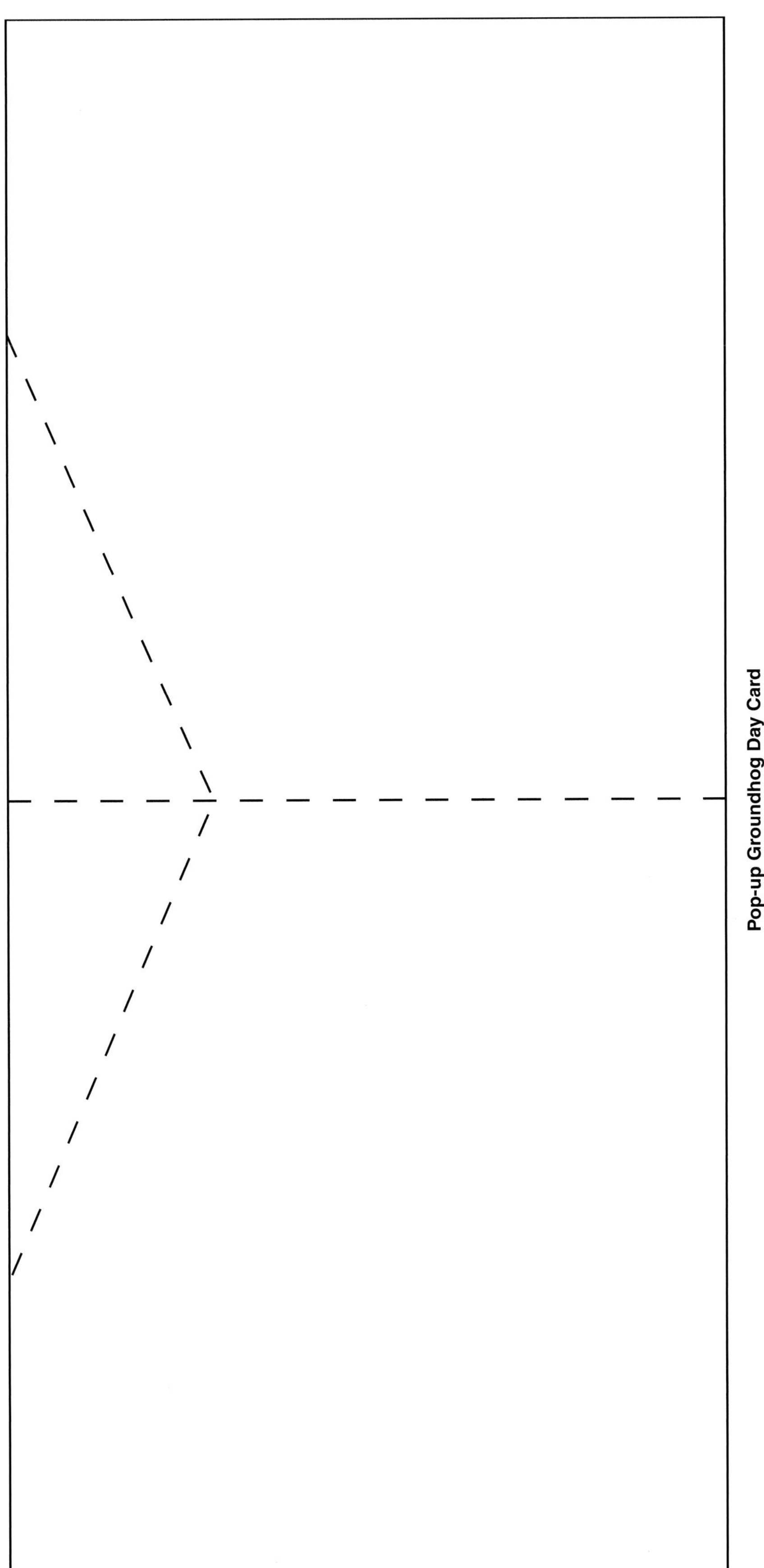

Pop-up Groundhog Day Card
Ground Rectangle
Cut on solid lines;
tear along top edge.
Score and fold on dashed lines.

Filigree Heart Container

CONTINUED FROM PAGE 31

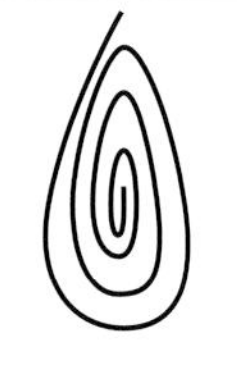

Filigree Heart Container
Teardrop

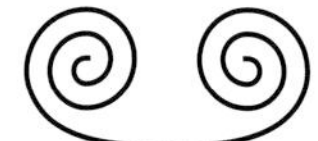

Filigree Heart Container
C Scroll

Measure of Love Gift Bag

CONTINUED FROM PAGE 33

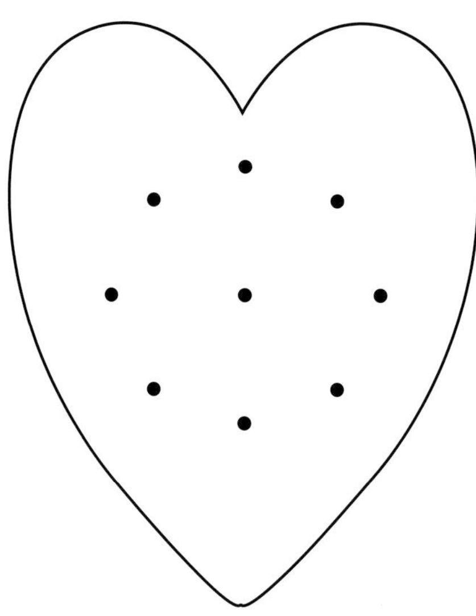

Measure of Love Gift Bag
Heart

Octopus Gift Bag

CONTINUED FROM PAGE 35

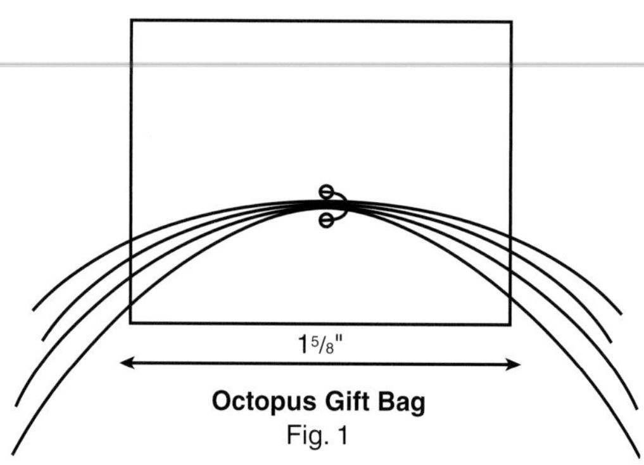

Octopus Gift Bag
Fig. 1

S.W.A.K. Gift Bag

CONTINUED FROM PAGE 36

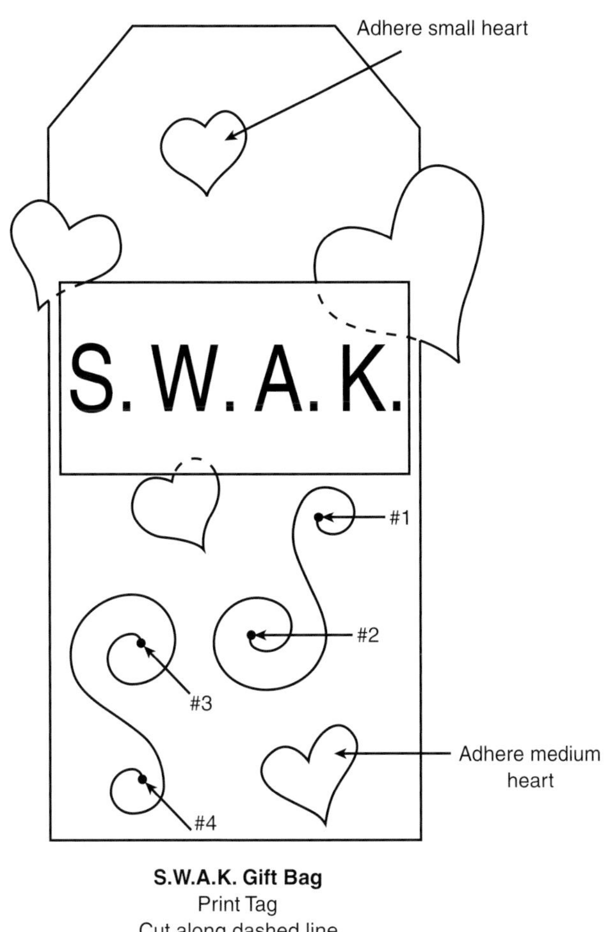

S.W.A.K. Gift Bag
Print Tag
Cut along dashed line

Pig Cookie Canister

CONTINUED FROM PAGE 39

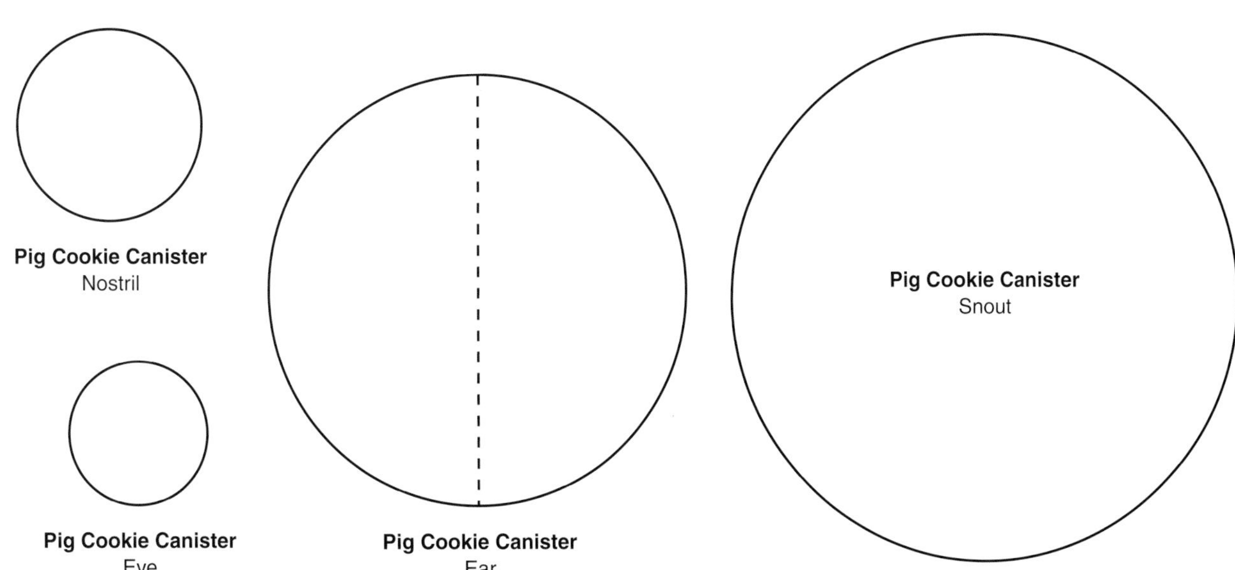

Pig Cookie Canister
Nostril

Pig Cookie Canister
Eye

Pig Cookie Canister
Ear

Pig Cookie Canister
Snout

Kiss Me, I'm Irish! Frame

CONTINUED FROM PAGE 43

Kiss Me, I'm Irish! Frame
Teardrop

Kiss Me, I'm Irish! Frame
Stem

Mini Lucky Album

CONTINUED FROM PAGE 45

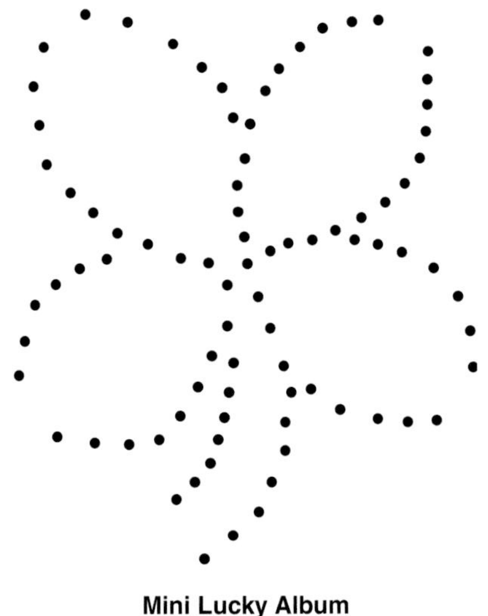

Mini Lucky Album
Shamrock

St. Patrick's Day Candy Box

CONTINUED FROM PAGE 47

St. Patrick's Day Candy Box
Pot

Easter Greetings Bucket

CONTINUED FROM PAGE 51

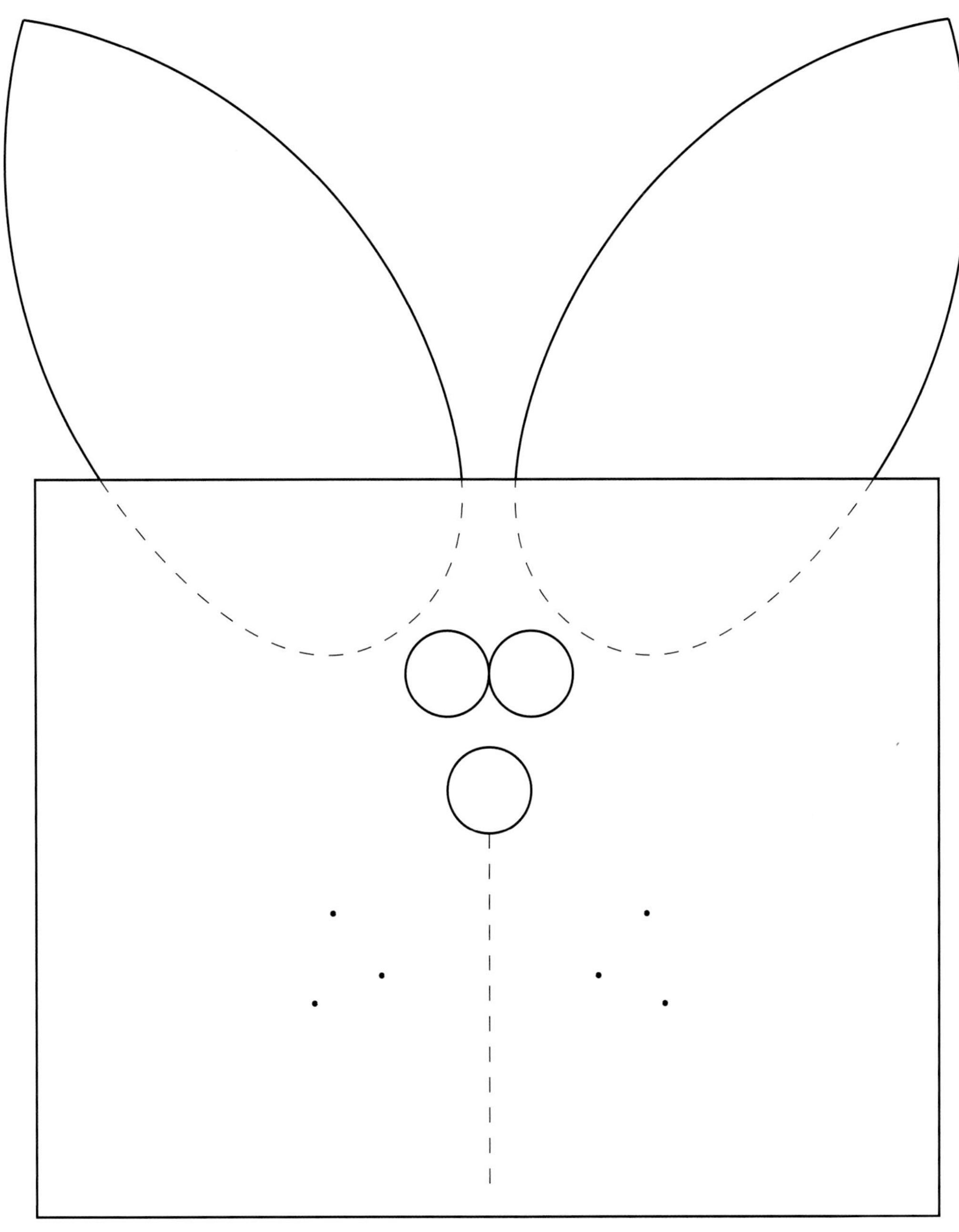

Easter Greetings Bucket
Bunny Head

Easter Egg Gift Set

CONTINUED FROM PAGE 52

Trim five remaining pink checked strips an inch or so longer than the long sides of the box. Weave them through the solid pink strips on one long side. Repeat on the other long side. Trim five remaining solid pink strips a little longer than short ends of the box; weave them through the pink checked strips on ends.

Trim all sides so that edges will fit together at corners, leaving strips on long sides longer so that ends can be folded around corners and glued under shorter strips. Assemble basket, adhering strips with instant-dry glue. Trim top edge of basket even. Slide basket off box.

Thread needle with yellow raffia. Sew blanket stitch over top edge of basket, stitching through openings between strips. Adhere raffia ends inside basket with instant-dry paper glue.

Using pattern provided and paper piercer, punch holes for three tulips on front of basket. ***Note:*** *Each flower is one strip wide. Bottom of stem is at bottom of basket; top row of holes should be just below second horizontal strip from top. The "holes" at the tops of the leaves and at the tops of the outer tulip petals—open circles on pattern—are actually openings between the woven paper strips; they do not need to be punched.*

Thread needle with green raffia. Stitch stems with backstitch; stitch leaves with long stitches, passing over each leaf twice. Adhere ends of raffia inside basket with instant-dry paper glue. Thread needle with pink raffia; stitch petals with straight stitches. ***Note:*** *Stitch bottoms of petals through hole at top of stem.* Adhere ends of raffia inside basket with instant-dry glue.

Punch a hole in each end of basket, ¾ inch below top edge. Set yellow eyelets in holes. Twist pink and yellow wires together; thread ends through eyelets. Adjust length of handle and twist wire ends to secure; trim with wire cutters. Tie yellow raffia around handle in a bow. Fill basket with crinkled pink paper shreds.

MINI EGG ALBUM

Fold yellow corrugated paper in half with grooves running lengthwise. Lay the 4 x 3-inch oval template on corrugated paper with template extending ⅛ inch beyond fold. Cut through both layers to make egg-shaped cover for album, leaving folded edge uncut.

Using pattern provided and paper piercer, punch holes for egg decoration on front cover. Using needle and pink raffia, stitch zigzag design through holes. Adhere raffia ends inside card with instant-dry glue. Using the 3½ x 2½-inch oval template, cut two ovals from pink checked paper. Adhere checked ovals inside covers with permanent adhesive. Let dry. Punch hole in front cover near edge opposite fold. Punch matching hole in back cover. Mount yellow eyelets in holes.

Fold white paper in half. Lay the 3½ x 2½-inch oval template on white paper with template extending ¾ inch beyond fold. Cut through both layers to make a joined pair of pages. Repeat to make a total of four pairs of pages.

Open pages and stack with edges even; position inside open corrugated cover. Using paper piercer, punch three holes down spine, through pages and cover. Thread needle with fine white cotton cord; stitch pages and cover together, knotting ends in middle of album. Secure knot with a drop of instant-dry paper glue; let dry, then trim ends of cord.

Cut fine yellow cord in half; knot one piece through each eyelet. Secure knots with a drop of instant-dry paper glue; let dry, then trim ends. Trim cords to 5 inches; knot ends. Close album by tying cords in a bow. ■

SOURCES: Wire from Toner Plastics; adhesives from Beacon.

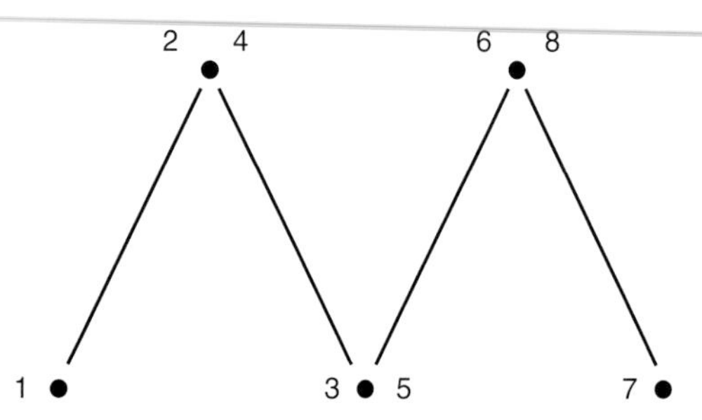

Easter Egg Gift Set
Mini Egg Album

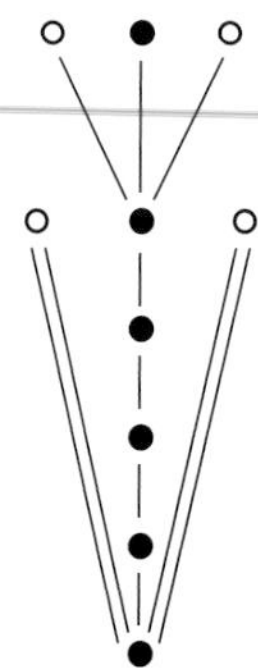

Easter Egg Gift Set
Easter Basket

Mother's Day Gift Set

CONTINUED FROM PAGE 69

Mother's Day Gift Set
Pouch Hat Brim

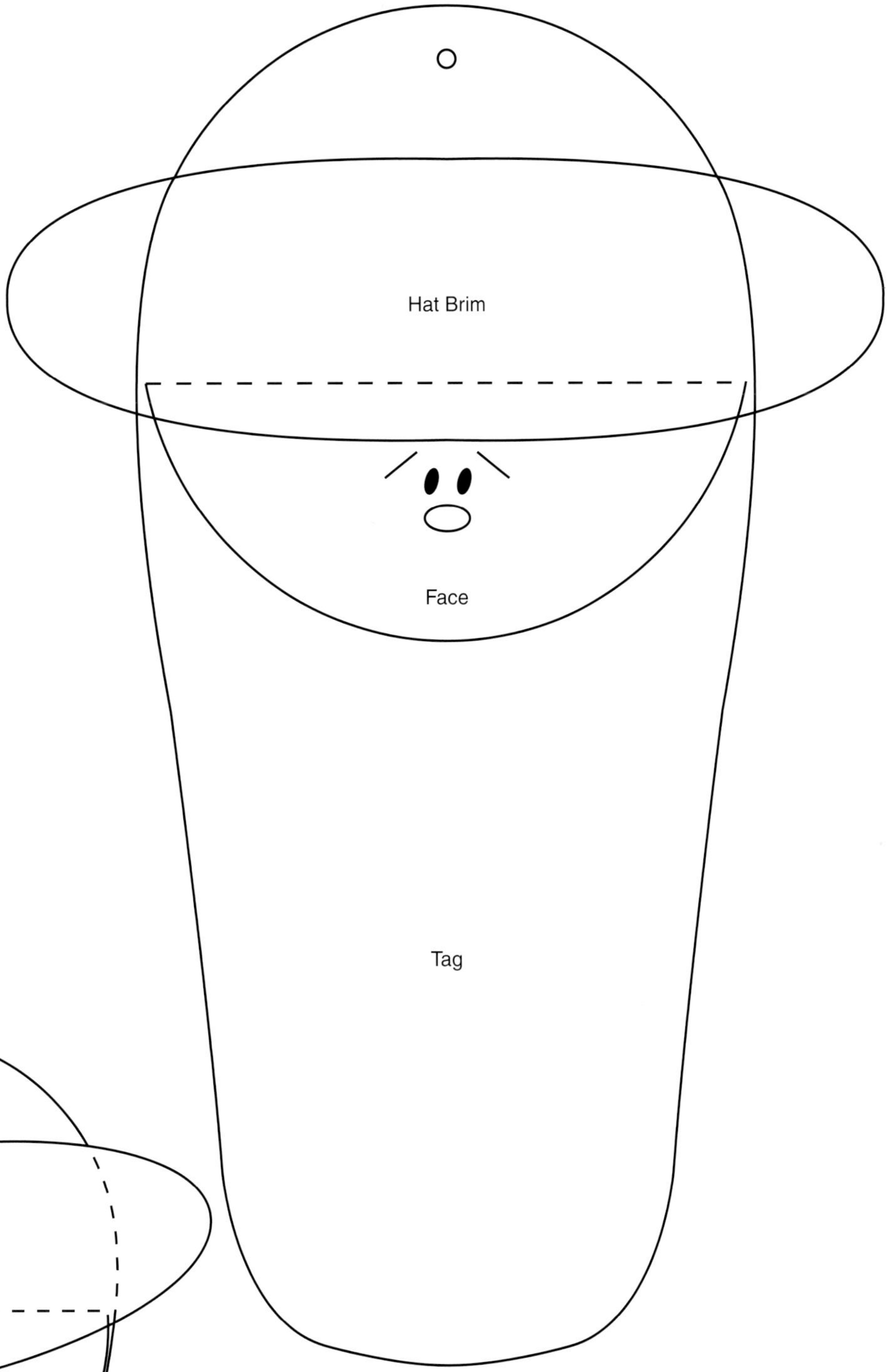

Hat Brim

Face

Tag

Mother's Day Gift Set
Tag

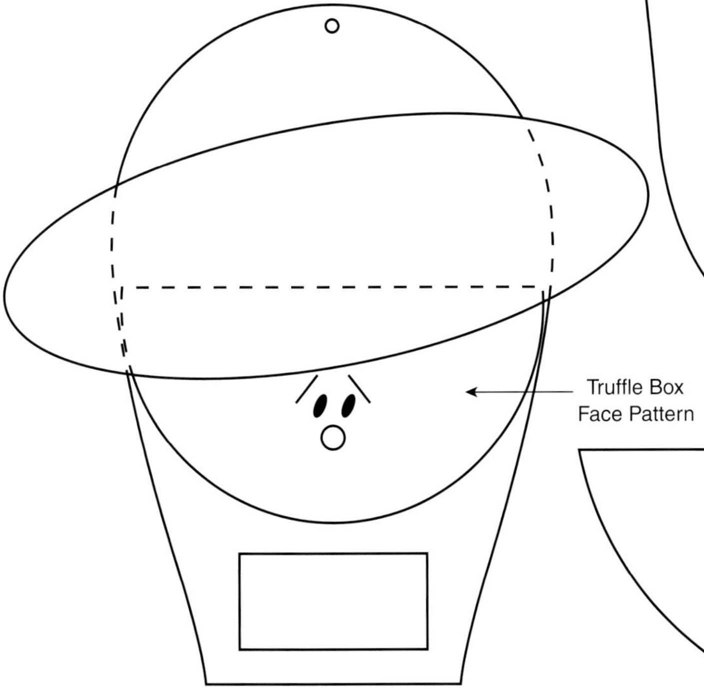

Truffle Box
Face Pattern

Mother's Day Gift Set
Truffle Box Assembly Diagram

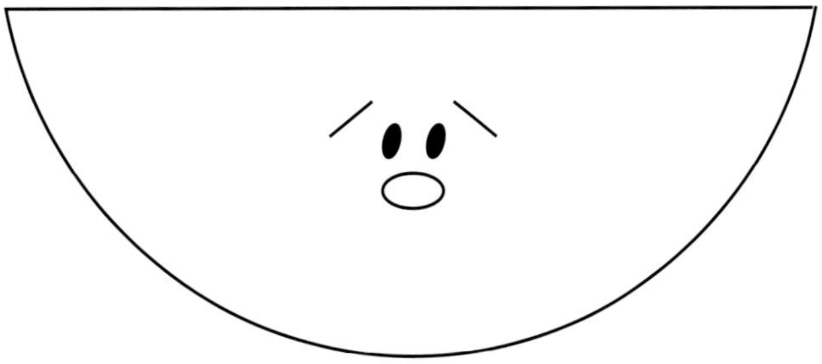

Mother's Day Gift Set
Pouch Face

Enlarge 110%

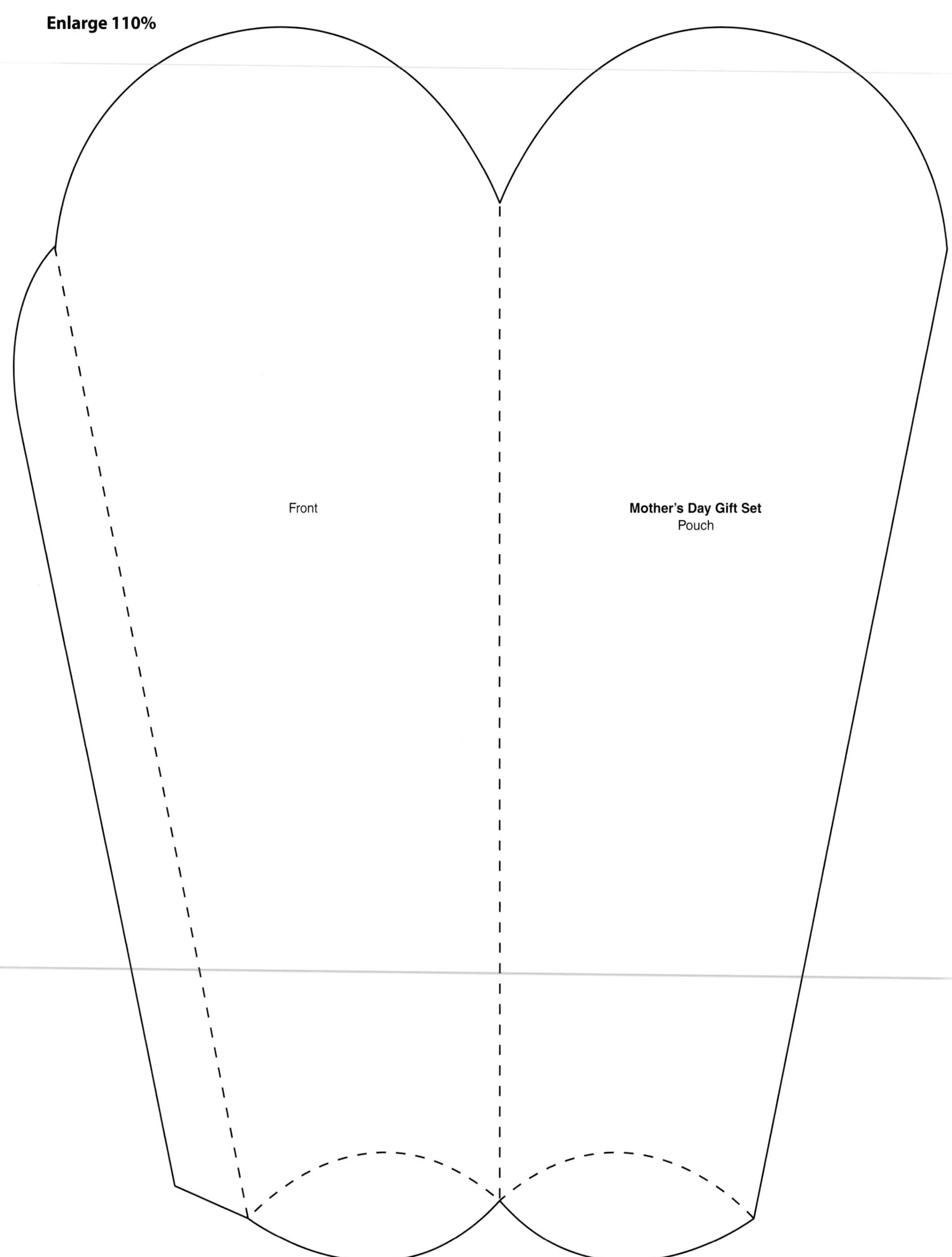

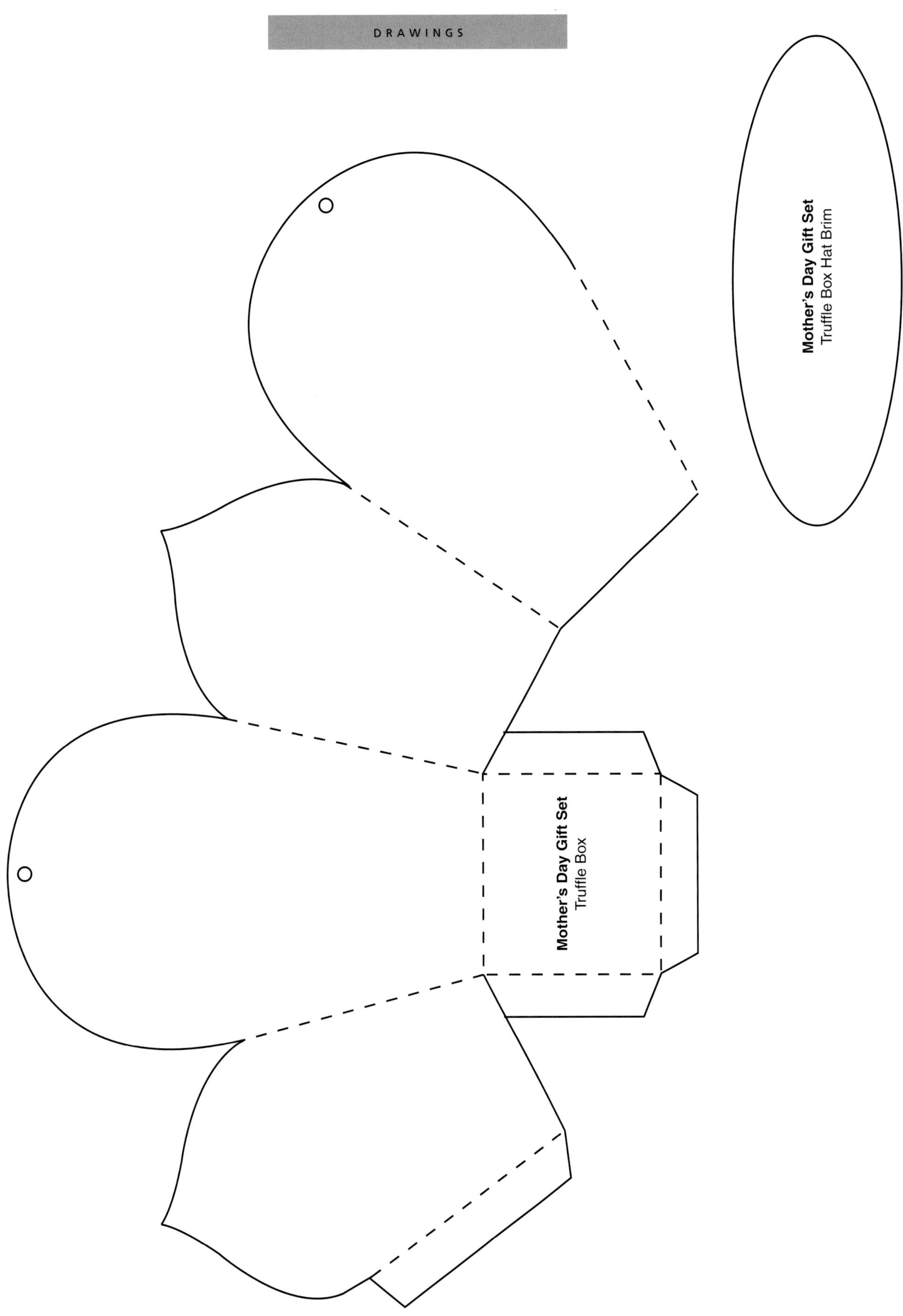
Mother's Day Gift Set
Truffle Box Hat Brim
Mother's Day Gift Set
Truffle Box

Graduation Card

CONTINUED FROM PAGE 73

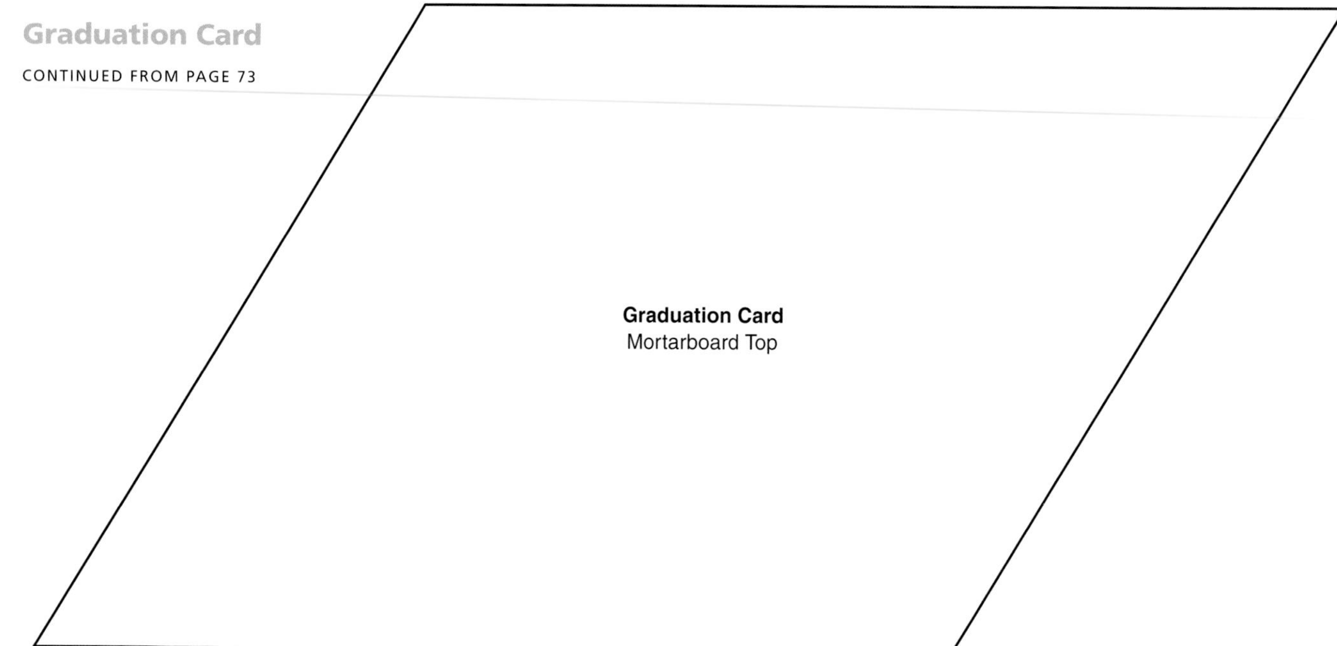

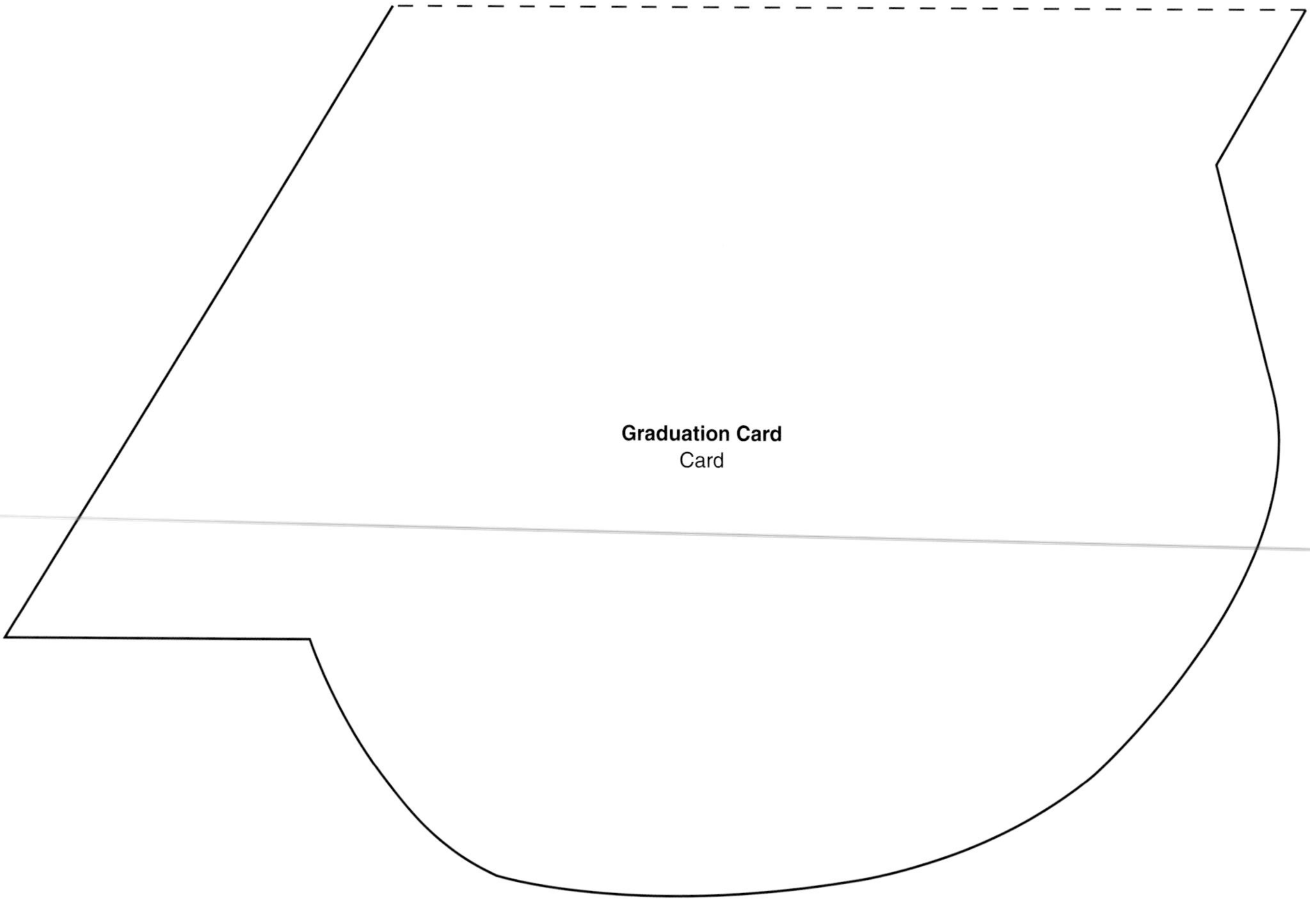

Graduation Card
Card

Floral Address Book

CONTINUED FROM PAGE 98

Cut three 6¾-inch lengths of fiber; lay them side by side down front cover, ¼ inch from spine. Fold ends over top and bottom edges; adhere inside cover. Repeat on back cover, positioning fibers where pale pink and rose card stocks meet.

Cut two 5⅝ x ⅝-inch strips rose card stock; adhere one inside each cover, near spine, to cover ends of fibers.

Tear two 2 x 1½-inch squares of rose card stock; center and mount a rose punch-out on each using adhesive dots, catching the end of a 1¼-inch length of fiber under each adhesive dot. Center and mount rose panels inside covers.

Lightly chalk the edges of cover and the spine. Adhere alphabet stickers to spell "Addresses" on front cover. Adhere quotation sticker on a small rectangle of pale pink card stock; mat it on rose card stock, then again on pale pink, leaving narrow borders. Adhere on front cover in lower left corner.

String charm on fiber; wrap around lower right corner of framed roses punch-out; secure using adhesive dots. Adhere entire piece in lower right corner of front cover using adhesive dots.

Stamp rose on back cover using foam stamp and deep pink ink pad. When dry, adhere quotation sticker over stamped rose. Tie 4-inch strand of fiber in a bow; adhere to sticker using glue dots. ■

SOURCES: Quotation stickers from Cloud 9 Design; alphabet stickers from NRN Designs.

Teacher's Mini Album

CONTINUED FROM PAGE 113

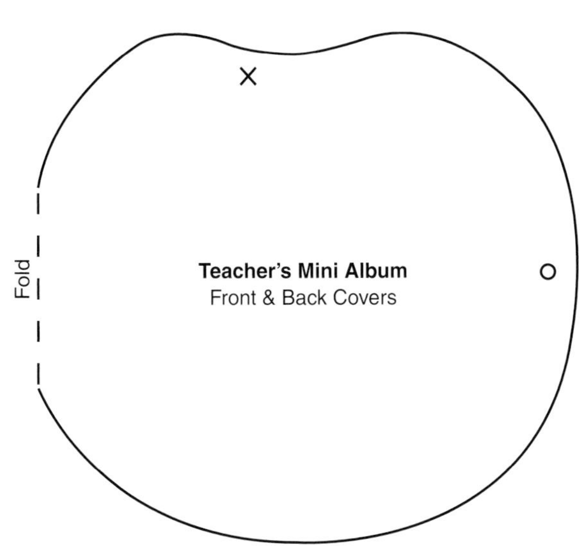

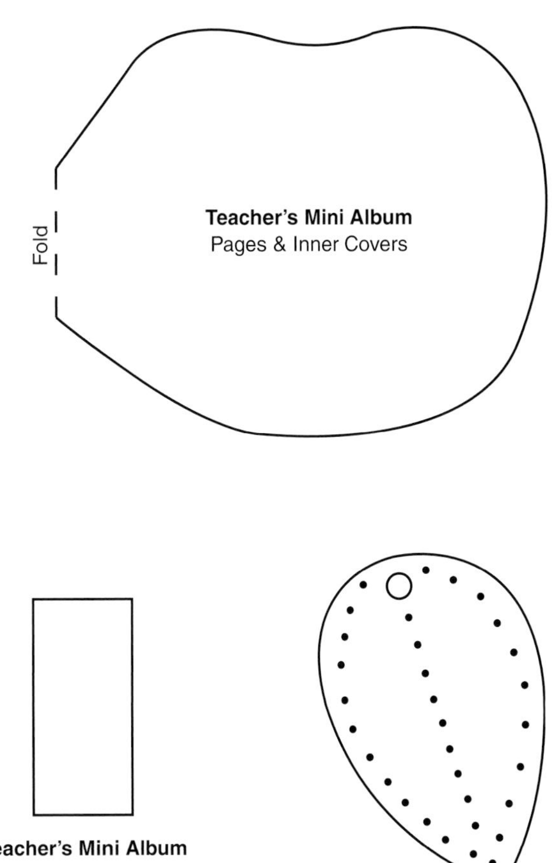

Princess Gift Set

CONTINUED FROM PAGE 107

Altered CD

Thoroughly sand surface of CD with sandpaper so that glue will adhere. Cut a circle of pink patterned paper to cover CD; adhere to front using paper glue. Ink edges using purple ink pad.

Wrap fiber across CD 1½ inches from top; adhere ends on back using adhesive dots. Adhere hat, "PRINCESS," mirror, purse and flower cutouts to CD using adhesive dots and adhesive foam dots. Adhere strands of fiber to back of hat at tip using adhesive dots.

Select alphabet tags to spell name; adhere to CD using adhesive foam dots. Clip a clothespin to fiber to "hold" each tag; adhere clothespins to CD using adhesive dots. Adhere tiara overlapping first letter using adhesive dot.

Cut a circle of white card stock to cover back of CD; adhere using paper glue. Hot glue a clothespin to back of CD. ***Option:*** *Adhere an adhesive-backed magnet strip to back of CD.* ■

SOURCES: Patterned paper from Provo Craft; paper cutouts from PM Designs; chalk ink pad by Clearsnap.

MATERIALS

- CD
- Pink patterned paper
- White card stock
- Princess-theme color paper cutouts
- Alphabet tags
- 1-inch spring clothespins
- Decorative fibers
- Purple chalk ink pad
- Fine sandpaper
- Adhesive-backed magnet strip (optional)
- Paper glue
- Adhesive dots
- Adhesive foam dots
- Hot-glue gun and glue stick

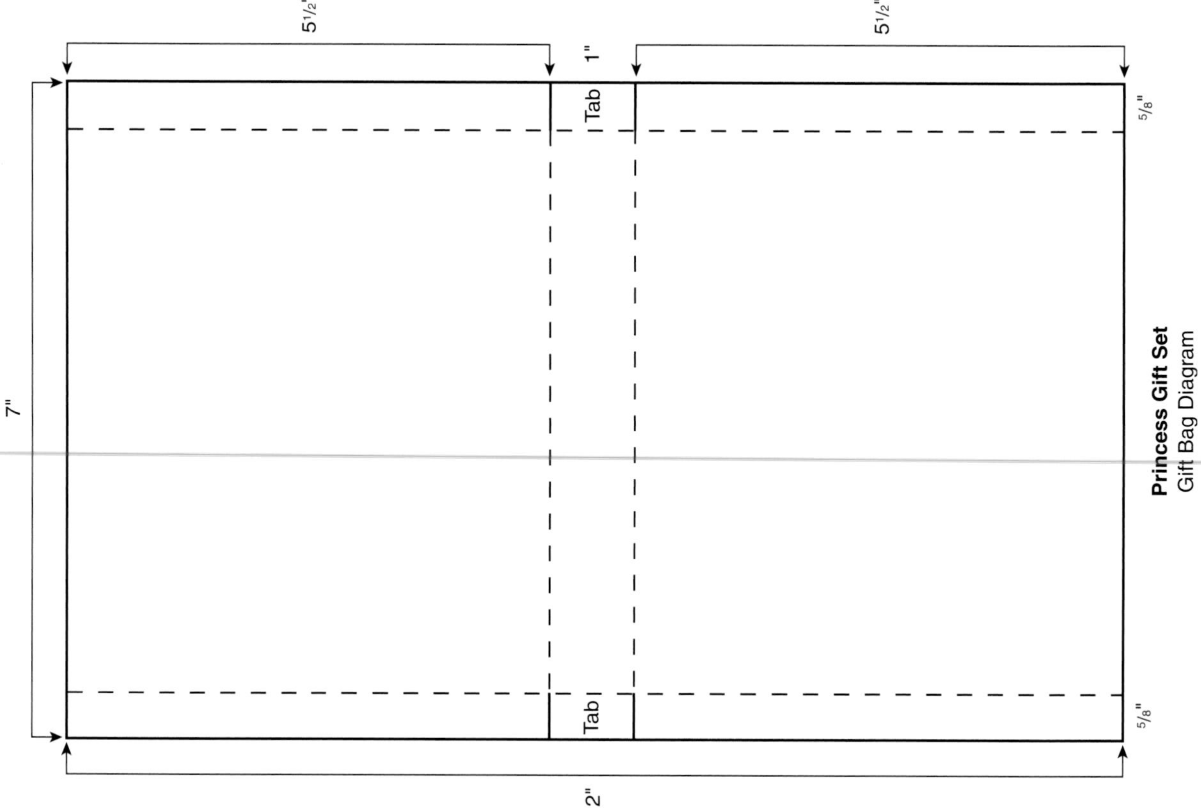

Ornament & Pine Branch Plaques

CONTINUED FROM PAGE 139

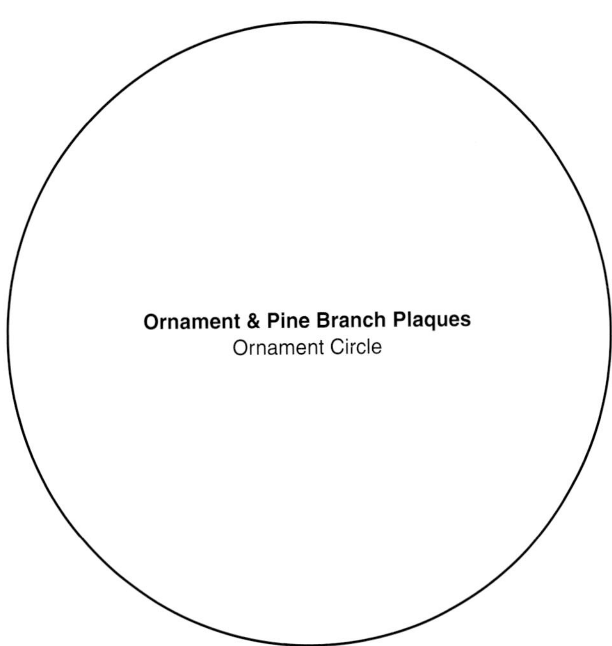

Christmas Holly Leaf Jar

CONTINUED FROM PAGE 140

Use computer or hand print "have a holly jolly Christmas" on vellum. Tear a 1 x 2¼-inch rectangle around words. Position rectangle in lower right corner of gold square; punch 1⁄16-inch holes through all layers and attach vellum to gold square with brads.

Center and punch a ⅛-inch hole near each side edge of gold square; set eyelets in holes. Thread green-and-white striped ribbon through eyelets; tie paper to jar, tying ribbon ends in a bow on left side. Trim and notch ribbon ends.

Use computer or hand print "celebrate" on vellum. Cut a 1 x 3½-inch rectangle around word, positioning word toward left. Rub edges with gold ink pad. Tear a 1½ x 4-inch rectangle from green card stock; center and adhere vellum to green card stock. Using sewing machine and gold thread, zigzag around vellum.

Punch a ⅛-inch hole near right edge of vellum and card stock; set eyelet in hole. Thread red-and-white checked ribbon through eyelet; tie tag around edge of lid, tying ends in a bow on front of tag. Trim ribbon ends. ■

SOURCES: Spray paint from Krylon; Fabri-Tac adhesive from Beacon.

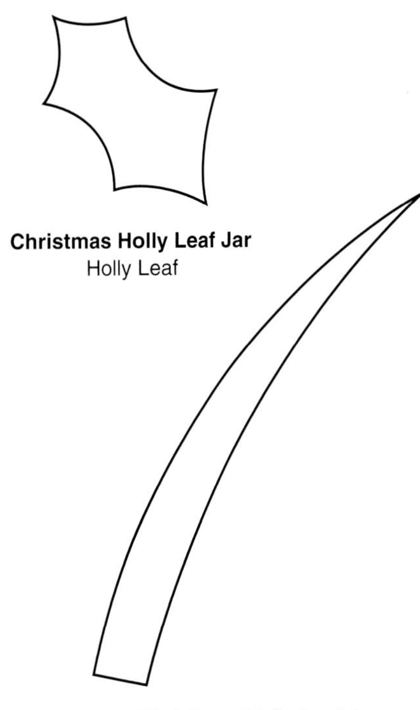

Golden Star Bag

CONTINUED FROM PAGE 143

Golden Star Bag
Star

White Poinsettia Frame

CONTINUED FROM PAGE 153

White Poinsettia Frame
Poinsettia Top Layer

White Poinsettia Frame
Marquis

White Poinsettia Frame
Triangle

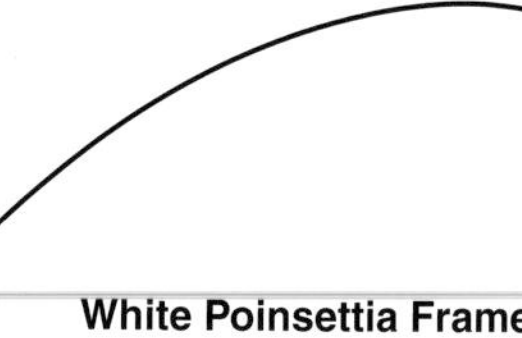

White Poinsettia Frame
Curled Stem

White Poinsettia Frame
Placement Diagram
Bottom Layer

General Instructions

Paper crafting is easy, creative and fun. Collect basic tools and supplies, learn a few simple terms and techniques, and you're ready to start. The possibilities abound!

Cutting & Tearing

Craft knife, cutting mat Must-have tools. Mat protects work surface, keeps blades from getting dull.

Measure and mark Diagrams show solid lines for cutting, dotted lines for folding.

Other cutters Guillotine and rotary-blade paper cutters, oval and circle cutters, cutters that cut unusual shapes via a gear or cam system, swivel-blade knives that cut along the channels of plastic templates, and die-cutting machines (large or small in size and price). Markers that draw as they cut.

Punches Available in hundreds of shapes and sizes ranging from 1/16 inch to over 3 inches (use for eyelets, lettering, dimensional punch art, and embellishments). Also punches for two-ring, three-ring, coil, comb and disk binding.

Scissors Long and short blades that cut straight or a pattern. Scissors with nonstick coating are ideal for cutting adhesive sheets and tape, bonsai scissors are best for cutting rubber or heavy board. Consider comfort—large holes for fingers, soft grips.

Tearing Tear paper for collage, special effects, layering on cards, scrapbook pages and more. Wet a small paintbrush; tear along the wet line for a deckle edge.

Embellishments

If you are not already a pack rat, it is time to start! Embellish projects with stickers, eyelets, brads, nail heads, wire, beads, iron-on ribbon and braid, memorabilia and printed ephemera.

Embossing

Dry embossing Use a light source, stencil, card stock and stylus tool. Add color, or leave raised areas plain.

Heat embossing Use embossing powder, ink, card stock and a heat tool to create raised designs and textures. Powders come in a wide range of colors. Fine grain is called "detail" and heavier is called "ultrathick." Embossing powders will not stick to most dye inks—use pigment inks or special clear embossing inks for best results.

Glues & Adhesives

Basics Each glue or adhesive is formulated for a particular use and specified surfaces. Read the label and carefully follow directions, especially those that involve personal safety and health.

Foam tape adds dimension.

Glue dots, adhesive sheets and cartridge type machines quick grab, no drying time needed.

Glue pens Fine line control.

Glue sticks Wide coverage.

Repositionable products Useful for stencils and temporary holding.

Measuring

Rulers A metal straightedge for cutting with a craft knife is a must-have tool. Match the length of the ruler to the project (shorter rulers are easier to use when working on smaller projects).

Quilter's grid ruler Use to measure squares and rectangles.

Paper & Card Stock

Card stock Heavier and stiffer than paper. A sturdy surface for cards, boxes, ornaments.

Paper Lighter-weight surfaces used for drawing, stamping, collage.

Storage and organization Store paper flat and away from moisture. Arrange by color, size or type. Keep your scraps for collage projects.

Types Handmade, milled, marbled, mulberry, origami, embossed, glossy, matte, botanical inclusions, vellum, parchment, preprinted, tissue and more.

Pens & Markers

Choose inks (permanent, watercolor, metallic, etc.), **colors** (sold by sets or individually), **and nibs** (fine point, calligraphy, etc.) to suit the project. For journals and scrapbooks, make sure inks are permanent and fade-resistant.

Store pens and markers flat unless the manufacturer says otherwise.

Scoring & Folding

Folding Mountain folds—up, valley folds—down. Most patterns will have different types of dotted lines to denote mountain or valley folds.

Tools Scoring tool and bone folder. Fingernails will scar the surface of the paper.

Stamping

Direct-to-paper (DTP) Use ink pad, sponge or stylus tool to apply ink instead of a rubber stamp.

Inks Available in pads and re-inker bottles. Types include dye and pigment, permanent, waterproof and fade resistant or archival, chalk finish, fast drying, slow drying, rainbow and more. Read the labels to determine what is best for a project or surface.

Make stamps Carve rubber, erasers, carving blocks, vegetables. Heat Magic Stamp foam blocks to press against textures. Stamp found objects such as leaves and flowers, keys and coins, etc.

Stamps Sold mounted on wood, acrylic or foam, or unmounted (rubber part only), made from vulcanized rubber, acrylic or foam.

Store Flat and away from light and heat.

Techniques Tap the ink onto the stamp (using the pad as the applicator) or tap the stamp onto the ink pad. Stamp with even hand pressure (no rocking) for best results. For very large stamps, apply ink with a brayer. Color the surface of a stamp with watercolor markers (several colors), huff with breath to keep the colors moist, then stamp; or lightly spray with water mist before stamping for a very different effect.

Unmounted stamps Mount temporarily on acrylic blocks with Scotch Poster Tape on one surface (nothing on the rubber stamp) or one of the other methods (hook and loop, paint on adhesives, cling plastic).

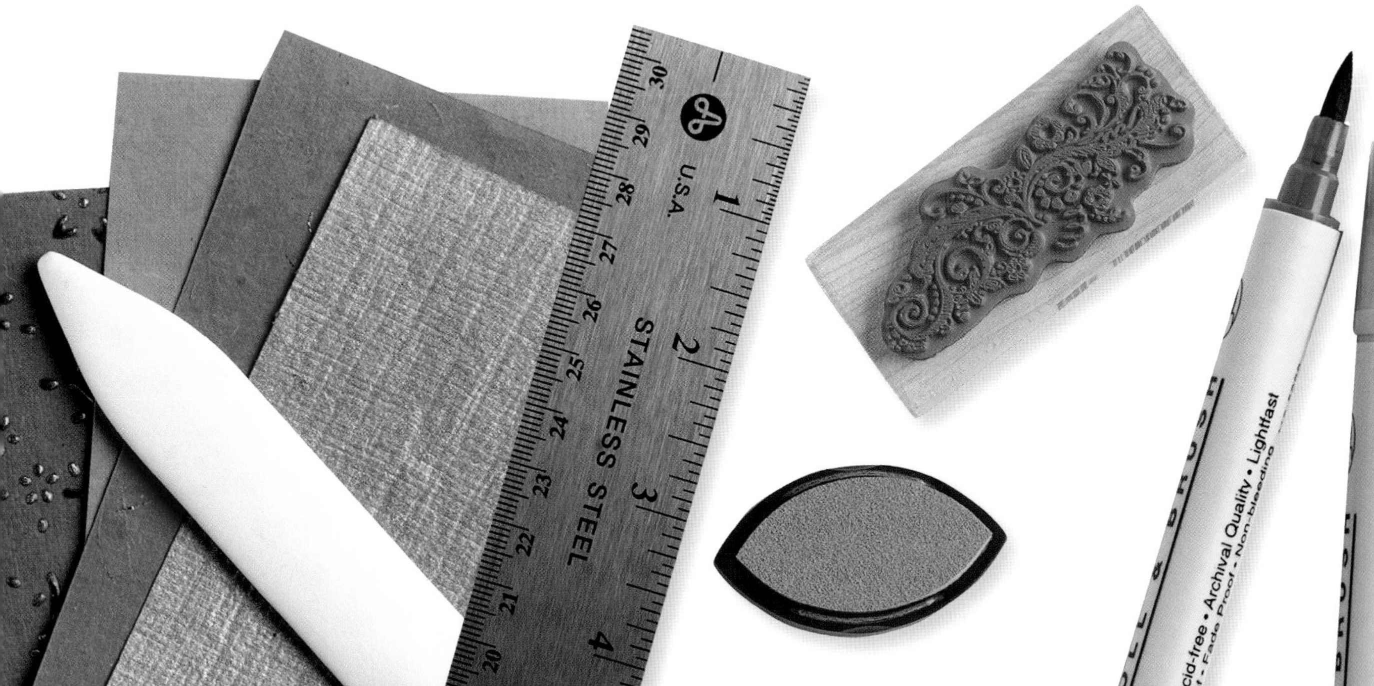

Buyer's Guide

Projects in this book were made using products provided by the manufacturers listed below. Look for the suggested products in your local craft- and art-supply stores. If unavailable, contact suppliers below. Some may be able to sell products directly to you; others may be able to refer you to retail sources.

Note: *Phone numbers and Web addresses are subject to change without notice.*

7gypsies
(877) 749-7797
www.sevengypsies.com

A Stamp in the Hand
(310) 884-9700
www.astampinthe hand.com

Aldik
(800) 442-5345
www.aldik.com

All My Memories
(888) 553-1998
www.allmymemories.com

Altered Pages
www.alteredpages.com

American Art Clay Co. Inc.
(317) 244-6871
www.amaco.com

American Crafts
(801) 226-0747
www.americancrafts.com

American Science & Surplus
(847) 647-0011
www.sciplus.com

Artistic Wire Ltd.
(630) 530-7567
www.artisticwire.com

Autumn Leaves
(800) 588-6707
www.autumnleaves.com

BasicGrey
(801) 544-1116
www.basicgrey.com

Beacon Adhesives Inc.
(914) 699-3400
www.beaconcreates.com

Blue Moon Beads
(800) 377-6715
www.bluemoon beads.com

Bo-Bunny Press
www.bobunny.com

Carolee's Creations & Co.
(435) 563-1100
www.carolees creations.com

Chatterbox
(208) 939-9133
www.chatterboxinc.com

Clearsnap Inc.
(888) 448-4862
www.clearsnap.com

Close To My Heart
(888) 655-6552
www.closetomyheart.com

Colorbök
(734) 424-0505
www.colorbok.com

CPE/The Felt Co.
(800) 327-0059
www.cpe-felt.com

Craf-T Products
(507) 235-3996
www.craf-tproducts.com

Creative Imaginations
(714) 500-1200
www.cigift.com

Creative Impressions
(719) 596-4860
www.creative-impressions.com

Creative Paperclay Co. Inc.
(805) 484-6648
www.paperclay.com

Daisy D's Paper Co.
(888) 601-8955
www.daisydspaper.com

Delta Technical Coating Inc./Rubber Stampede
(800) 423-4135
www.deltacrafts.com

Deluxe Designs
(480) 497-9005
www.deluxecuts.com

DeNami Design
(253) 437-1626
www.denamidesign.com

Design Originals
(817) 877-0067
www.d-originals.com

Designs by Loretta
www.designsby loretta.com

DieCuts with a View
(801) 224-6766
www.diecutswith aview.com

DMD Inc.
(800) 805-9890
www.dmdind.com

Doodlebug Design Inc.
(801) 966-9952
www.doodlebug designinc.com

Duncan Enterprises
(800) 438-6226
www.duncan-enter prises.com

DYMO Corp.
global.dymo.com

Eclectic Products
(800) 693-4667
www.eclectic products.com

EK Success Ltd.
(973) 458-0092
www.eksuccess.com

Eyelet Queen/ Queen & Co.
(858) 485-5132
www.eyeletqueen.com

Fiskars Brands Inc.
(800) 500-4849
www.fiskars.com

Frances Meyer Inc.
(912) 748-5252
www.francesmeyer.com

Golden Artist Colors Inc.
(800) 959-6543
www.goldenpaints.com

Halcraft USA
(212) 376-1580
www.halcraft.com

Hero Arts Rubber Stamps
(510) 652-6055
www.heroarts.com

Hot Off The Press/Paper Wishes
(888) 300-3406
www.craftpizazz.com

Impress Rubber Stamps,
www.impress rubberstamps.com

Inkadinkado
(800) 523-8452
www.inkadinkado.com

Jacquard Products: Rupert, Gibbon & Spider Inc.
(800) 442-0455
www.jacquard products.com

Jesse James & Co. Inc
(610) 435-7899
www.dressitup.com

Jest Charming Embellishments
(702) 564-5101
www.jestcharming.com

JudiKins
(310) 515-1115
www.judikins.com

Junkitz
(732) 792-1108
www.junkitz.com

K&Company
(816) 389-4150
www.kandcompany.com

Kangaroo and Joey
www.kangarooand joey.com

Karen Foster Design
(801) 451-9779
www.scrapbook paper.com

Kay
(858) 277-6798
www.paperand petalsbykay.com

KI Memories
(972) 243-5595
www.kimemories.com

Krylon/Sherwin-Williams Co.
(800) 4KRYLON
www.krylon.com

LazerLetterz
www.lazerletterz.com

Li'l Davis Designs
(949) 838-0344
www.lildavisdesigns.com

Magenta
(450) 922-5253
www.magentastyle.com

Magic Mesh
www.mypajamason.com

Magic Scraps
(972) 238-1838
www.magicscraps.com

Making Memories
(801) 294-0430
www.making memories.com

me & my BIG ideas
www.meandmybig ideas.com

Memories Complete
(801) 492-1992
www.memoriescomplete.com

Mrs. Grossman's Paper Co.
(800) 429-4549
www.mrsgrossmans.com

Mustard Moon
www.mustardmoon.com

Northwoods Rubber Stamps
(651) 430-0816
www.northwoods rubberstamps.com

NRN Designs
(714) 898-6363
www.nrndesigns.com

Paper Adventures
(414) 645-5760
www.paper adventures.com

Paper Fever Inc.
www.paperfever.com

Paper Inspirations Inc.
(406) 756-9677
www.paper inspirations.com

The Paper Loft
www.paperloft.com

Pebbles Inc.
(801) 224-1857
www.pebblesinc.com

Penny Black Inc.
www.pennyblackinc.com

Petals & Possibilities/ Pressed Petals
(800) 748-4656
www.pressedpetals.com

Pinecone Press
(714) 434-9881
www.pineconepress books.com

Pixie Press/Darice
(800) 321-1494, ext. 3229
www.pixiepress.com

Plaid/All Night Media
(800) 842-4197
www.plaidonline.com

PM Designs
(888) 595-2887
www.designsbypm.com

PrintWorks Collection Inc.
(562) 906-1262
www.printworks collection.com

Provo Craft
(800) 563-8679
www.creativexpress.com

The Punch Bunch
(254) 791-4209
www.thepunch bunch.com

QuicKutz Inc.,
(801) 765-1144
www.quickutz.com

Ranger Industries Inc.
(732) 389-3535
www.rangerink.com

Royal & Langnickel Brush Mfg. Inc.
(800) 247-2211
www.royalbrush.com

Rubber Stamp Ave.
(541) 665-9981
www.rubberstamp ave.com

Rusty Pickle
(801) 746-1045
www.rustypickle.com

Scrap a Latte
www.scrapalatte.net

Scrapworks,
(801) 363-1010
www.scrapworks.com

ScrapYard
(866) 242-2742
www.scrapyard329.com

SEI
(800) 333-3279
www.shopsei.com

Sizzix/Ellison
(877) 355-4766

Stampabilities
(800) 888-0321 ext. 1238
www.stampabilities.com

Stampendous
(714) 688-0288
www.stampendous.com

Stampers Anonymous, div. of Art Gone Wild & Friends
(800) 945-3980
www.stampers anonymous.com

Stampin' Up!
(800)-STAMPUP
www.stampinup.com

Sticker Studio
(208) 322-2465
www.stickerstudio.com

Sweetwater,
(970) 867-4428
www.sweetwater scrapbook.com

The Designer's Library
(660) 582-6484
www.thedesigners library.com

The Stamp Doctor
(866) 782-6737
www.stampdoctor.com

Tombow
(800) 835-3232
www.tombowusa.com

Toner Plastics Inc.
(413) 789-1300
www.tonerplastics.com

Treehouse Designs
(877) 372-1109
www.tree house-designs.com

Tsukineko Inc.
(800) 769-6633
www.tsukineko.com

Uchida of America
(800) 541-5877
www.uchida.com

Walnut Hollow
(800) 950-5101
www.walnuthollow.com

Wordsworth
(719) 282-3495
www.wordsworth stamps.com

Xyron
(800) 793-3523
www.xyron.com

Yellow Rose Art Stamps
(830) 606-6694
www.yellowroseart stamps.com

Designer Index

Index